BATHROOMS

Design *Is in the* Details

Brad Mee

Sterling Publishing Co., Inc. New York
A Sterling/Chapelle Book

Chapelle, Limited
Owner: Jo Packham
Editor: Karmen Potts Quinney
Cover Image: Kohler Co.

If you have any questions or comments, please contact:
Chapelle, Ltd., Inc., P.O. Box 9252 Ogden, UT 84409
(801) 621-2777 • FAX (801) 621-2788
• e-mail: chapelle@chapelleltd.com
• web site: www.chapelleltd.com

Due to differing conditions, tools, and individual skills, the publisher cannot be responsible for any injuries, losses, and/or other damage which may result from the use of the information in this book.

Library of Congress Cataloging-in-Publication Data Available

10 9 8 7 6 5 4 3 2

Published in paperback 2004 by Sterling Publishing Co., Inc.
387 Park Avenue South, New York, NY 10016

Distributed in Canada by Sterling Publishing
℅ Canadian Manda Group, 165 Dufferin Street,
Toronto, Ontario, Canada M6K 3H6
Distributed in Great Britain by Chrysalis Books Group PLC,
The Chrysalis Building, Bramley Road, London W10 6SP, England.
Distributed in Australia by Capricorn Link (Australia) Pty. Ltd.
P.O. Box 704, Windsor, NSW 2756, Australia
Printed in China

Sterling ISBN 1-4027-0060-1 Hardcover
ISBN 1-4027-1366-5 Paperback

For information about custom editions, special sales, premium and corporate purchases, please contact Sterling Special Sales Department at 800-805-5489 or specialsales@sterlingpub.com.

CONTENTS

INTRODUCTION 8

STYLE 10

spa style 12

luxury style 20

classic style 26

modern style 32

fantasy style 40

SHELL 46

walls 48

floors 56

ceilings 62

FIXTURES

bath

shower

sinks

66

68

78

88

EXTRAS 98

furniture 100

accessories 108

mirrors & lights 116

PURPOSE 120

powder room 122

his/hers 126

master bath 130

acknowledgments 138

credits 140

index 143

INTRODUCTION

To some, the ideal bathroom is an understated, quiet retreat, while for others, it's a luxurious space created for pure indulgence. Still others see it as an opportunity to create a dramatic room alive with theatrical design. In any case, today's bathroom has come a long way from the utilitarian cubbyhole designed solely for daily ablutions. Yesterday's out-of-the-way room predictably dressed with a plastic shower curtain and vinyl wallpaper has evolved into one of the most style-conscious spaces in the home.

As this formerly mundane room has blossomed, its area has expanded and become home to spectacular detail. In fact, the bathroom has become the most frequently redesigned and renovated room in today's home. Master baths often boast the square footage and accommodations of a second, albeit private, living room. Guest baths and powder rooms are lavished with stylish fixtures and head-turning ornamentation. Certainly, the bathroom has become a priority as people use it as their own sanctuary, escaping from the daily hustle and bustle both in and outside of the home. Along with this need to create a private getaway has come the desire to create a statement of style—a uniquely personalized space. This is where details enter, they are the finishing touches that give the bathroom a character and personality all its own.

Design elements once saved for showier and more highly appointed rooms in the home have reinvented the look of today's bathroom. Whether the room is shared with others, like a guest bath or powder room, or is a private, intimate space, the options for unique and personalized detail are endless. Starting with the basic fixtures and fittings (which don't look so basic anymore), choices include everything from extravagant flooring to beautiful furniture, dramatic lighting to distinctive accessories. Nothing is off-limits in today's newly defined bathroom. Color runs the gamut from softly soothing to brightly stimulating. Textures abound. Cool tile, grained woods, rough stone, and reflective glass all perfectly team with the room's other elements. Whether your preferred style is traditional or contemporary, spa-like or over-the-top, the options are countless.

As a room deserving distinctive character, the bathroom is truly exceptional. The uniqueness of the master bath, for example, is that it is not shared with or designed to impress guests or visitors. It is solely for the use and enjoyment of the home owners. It can, and should be, created for their pleasure alone. The powder room is normally small and used for short spurts of time. For these reasons, it can be host to extravagant and stunning details that are most impressive when enjoyed for a few moments but can become abrasive when experienced for a prolonged period. A guest or family bathroom invites detail that is warm and welcoming. This tempts the guest to linger a little longer, enjoy the privacy a little more. Regardless of the type of bathroom, the concept of the purely functional, characterless bathroom of the past has transcended through the generous use of distinctive detail.

Ultimately, the look and feel you bring to your bathroom should reflect your personal style and bring you a sense of comfort and exhilaration every time you enter the room. Throughout the following pages, you will find bathrooms that are alive with unique details. When you identify a look that you like, draw from it the elements of design that catch your eye. Let them inspire you to create your own private retreat, your personal version of the ideal bathroom.

STYLE

How would you describe the ultimate bathroom? Would it be an indulgent retreat with a large inviting tub and a spa-like atmosphere? Maybe you prefer a more theatrical style boasting bold colors and dramatic lighting. Or perhaps you like a classically appointed bathroom featuring a straightforward approach to its décor. Whatever look you prefer, each distinct style has a unique character that is created, in part, by recognizable details. Once you determine your preferred style, you can invite some or all these details into your own personalized bathroom. There are, of course, unlimited ways to mix and match details when creating your version of the ideal bathroom. And whether you are working on a new space or simply freshening up an existing bath, detail can turn your room into a haven brimming over with character. Further, as each individual detail is added, the personality of your ultimate bath becomes more clearly defined—one that is uniquely yours.

Experience the soft splash of water as you ease into a bath infused with scented oil. Feel cool tile underfoot and wrap yourself in a plush terry-cloth robe. Savor the quiet of the space and the fragrance of fresh eucalyptus or aromatic candles. Recline on a chaise and gaze out onto a private patio. This is the essence of the spa-style bathroom. It is an experience for all of the senses, a retreat for body and soul.

SPA STYLE

The room is designed not only to accommodate daily cleansing rituals but also to provide a private refuge in which to relax and unwind. It is not encumbered with heavy decoration or ornate accents. Instead, it relies on the beauty of natural materials, lighting, and understated details to create a calm, restorative haven in the home. The more elaborate and spacious spa-style baths pamper with whirlpool tubs, private saunas, and showers with massaging jet sprays. More modest bathrooms may incorporate one or more of these features, but also look to smaller, yet just as important, elements to create their relaxing environments. Marble, stone, wood, and simple tile become a backdrop to indulgent accents—thirsty cotton towels, hand-milled soaps, wood-handled bath accessories, fragrant oils, and lotions are just the beginning. Any detail that helps relax, rejuvenate, and recharge those who enjoy this tranquil space is at home in the spa-style bath.

Even the smallest bathrooms can borrow from an extravagant spa to create a peaceful atmosphere that relaxes and rejuvenates. They make use of every detail to bring pleasure. Calm, temperate shades are used to color the room—from tranquil blues and greens to peaceful whites and earth tones. A soothing mix of natural and ambient lighting is added to illuminate the room. Window coverings are left simple and patterns in the space are muted and kept to a minimum. Stainless-steel, glass, and translucent fixtures and accents are incorporated to mimic the relaxing, reflective properties of water. The tactile sensations offered by sisal floor mats, plush cotton towels, and an occasional accessory of cool stone or warm terra-cotta bring the room down to earth. Each detail that imitates and enhances the serene and therapeutic nature of water adds to the atmosphere of the spa-style bath.

PAGE 13
Clean lines, luminous surfaces, and an abundance of light bring a sense of serenity and calm to this brilliantly designed bathroom. The warm wood tones and texture-rich accents prevent the room from feeling cold or clinical.

UPPER LEFT
In endless ways, glass can be used to capture the lucent and soothing qualities of water. Here, iridescent glass tile, sleek accessories, and a sparkling transparent bowl add to the allure of this radiant lavatory.

LOWER LEFT
This timeless, tranquil bathroom derives its ambience from muted colors, cool marble, mosaic accents, and an irresistible overflow tub.

OPPOSITE
Water defines this spectacular bathroom as it flows from the ceiling to fill the bath and sprays and massages from multiple showerheads in both indoor and outdoor fixtures. Monochromatic stone surfaces and clean lines create the ideal backdrop for the spa-like space.

To be beautiful and be calm. . . is the ideal of nature.

Richard Jeffries

ABOVE
Nature is an integral part of this Japanese-style bath. It combines rich textures, diffused lighting, and symmetrically placed mirrors, sinks, and shower doors to create a calm, meditative space.

OPPOSITE LOWER LEFT
An enviable view, stone-tiled walls, and a Japanese-style sit-up wooden tub combine to create a sense of comfort and serenity in this small bathroom retreat.

OPPOSITE UPPER AND LOWER RIGHT
The interplay of texture-rich accents enhance any bath. Woven-straw slippers and plush towels are beautiful in their own right, but when combined, add considerably to the room's charm. Glowing bottles of body oils resting on woven mats conjure up images of relaxing massages in a warm, tropical setting.

The spa-style bathroom is the perfect home for the harmonious and healing essence of nature. By incorporating natural materials—the coolness of stone, the aroma of redwood, the texture-rich sensation of raw fibers—you can transform an everyday bathroom into an holistic retreat. Add to your physical experience by stocking the room with bath salts and herbal soaps. Reinvigorate with loofahs, natural-bristle brushes, and pumice stones. Pamper yourself with soothing ointments and oils. Wrap yourself in a thirsty robe, close your eyes, and enjoy the tranquility of the space.

Thousands have lived without love,
not one without water.

W. H. Auden

Life depends upon water; it is our most essential substance. In the bath, it touches us both physically and spiritually in its ability to cleanse, cool, and refresh. It is no wonder that the most natural and nurturing of bathroom styles—the spa style—often centers around water. In spa-style baths, large and small, inviting tubs and walk-in showers provide immediate and satisfying contact with water. Waterfall faucets, rain showerheads, and steam settings deepen the experience. The serene and refreshing nature of water is further enhanced with open floor space, natural light, and a generous use of glass, mirrors, and reflective hardware.

Is it a bathroom, sitting room, or second living room? The confusion is understandable. After all, here is a room with surfaces, finishes, and furnishings found in beautifully decorated living rooms and yet, there is also a tub, sink, and other required amenities of the standard bathroom. This is the nature of the luxury-style bath. One looks far beyond the requirements of a working bathroom to create a sumptuous, often decadent space in which to bathe, lounge, and simply escape the outside world. Softer than the spa style, the luxurious bathroom embraces detail that masks the

LUXURY STYLE

functional nature of the room and creates an elegant atmosphere that is soothing and comfortable. In the master bath, design elements are often drawn from the adjoining bedroom—thick carpeting, plush upholstered furniture, softly colored walls, shaded lamps, rich artwork, framed mirrors, flourishing plants, and artfully displayed accessories. The tub or nearby chaise may be flanked by an accent table offering a quiet place to curl up with a book or to phone a friend. Decanters of perfumed soaps, colorful bath beads, and silky oils allude to how time is best spent here. The home's guest bath and powder room are similarly appointed with rich decoration and posh details. What you won't find in the luxurious bath are medicine cabinets, robust accessories, hard lighting, or an abundance of natural materials or coarse textures. This room is not created to enervate or rejuvenate but, instead, to soothe and indulge its fortunate guests.

The luxury-style bath surrounds its guests with a rich and sumptuous ambience. It eschews anything that brazenly speaks of the practical nature of the bathroom, replacing it with a more stylized and indulgent element. Claw-footed tubs, walk-in showers, sculpted pedestal sinks, and chest-like vanities are preferred over more standard features. Faux-finished walls, patterned wallpaper, and beautifully framed mirrors add elegance. Elaborate window coverings and shower curtains soften even the hardest bathroom and rich, delicious colors enrich and warm the space. Refined hardware and distinctive accessories finish the bathroom beautifully.

PAGE 21
In this luxurious bath, detail flourishes to create an air of opulence. Rich, polished stone frames an expansive mirror. Lush plants, stately candle groupings, and a sumptuous leather sofa with faux animal-skin accessories cocoon the space with elegance and irresistible comfort.

RIGHT
Stunning marble and brilliant lighting combine to make this bathroom glow with style and sophistication. Attentive details—vertical interior shower-stall windows, lighted steps, oversized art, and a plush crescent-shaped sofa—all add to the room's alluring ambience.

Often, the best examples of the luxury-style bath can be found in fine hotels. After all, these bathrooms are created solely to coddle their guests. By incorporating some of the amenities found in these spaces—heated towel rack, telephone, television, lotion dispenser—you can turn your bathroom into your own four-star refuge. Don't be shy about incorporating nontraditional treatments and accents. Chandeliers, sumptuous furnishings, flickering candles, and lush plants, all add to the richness of the space while disguising its practical nature.

Style is a magic wand, and turns everything to gold it touches.

Logan Pearsall Smith

The bathroom should be filled with objects that make it a pleasure to use. The bath's accessories, and even its most basic necessities, can bring elegance and charm to the room through their own inherent beauty.

LEFT
A glamorous bench, ornately framed mirror and a collection of crystalline accents and sparkling accessories underscore the refined and rich tone of this space.

RIGHT AND BELOW
Look to the forms and finishes of the room's everyday amenities to add to its luxurious ambience. Hand towels, soap stands, sconces, and even a hairbrush and hand mirror are just a few examples of working accents that can be as beautiful as they are practical.

CLASSIC STYLE

Honest, timeless, soulful, . . . all words that characterize the classic-style bath. Devoid of pretense or overwhelming decoration, the classic bathroom relies on purity of form and finish to create its appeal. It is almost therapeutic in its simplicity. Clean lines, spare patterns, tranquil colors, and a lack of clutter create the room's natural beauty. The look has longevity; no passing fads or fashions fit here. Timeless designs and finishes are used. Surfaces are faced with tile, softly veined marble, or even beaded wainscoting. Porcelain reigns in the classic bath, as does white. A palette of pale hues or an understated spot of color are also at home here. The room's essential elements—tub, sink, shower, hardware, surfaces—strongly define its character. For this reason, an attention to detail and craftsmanship is devoted to each and every one of them. The curve of the tub, contour of the faucets, and even the lines of the towel rack, for example, shape the personality of the room. Each is stunning in its simplicity and valued in its contribution to the overall feel of the room. Period lighting fixtures, plain plush towels, and an assortment of functional accessories fit this room perfectly. A white ceramic soap dish, clear glass shelf, and curved chrome robe hook are only a few examples of the well-placed touches you may find. Superfluous artwork, knickknacks, or just-for-show objects are out of place. Tried and true, the classic style is a perennial favorite that brings ease and comfort to a room that should, after all, be just that.

Classic is the most straightforward of bath styles. It does not attempt to camouflage or redefine the room's purpose. Instead, it relies on integrity of design to create its appeal. "Is the piece functional, well made, and visually appealing?" is the question asked. For example, to the lover of the classic style, a soap dish is a ceramic, glass, or chrome tray that is simply styled and well designed to hold a bar of soap. It isn't an ornate crystal bowl, elaborately carved wooden block, or high-style plastic vessel. This same approach is used to evaluate every design element of the room—from tub to sink, surface treatments to accessories. For each, function precedes form and selection is based on fine workmanship, classic lines, and timeless beauty. When combined, the components create an honest room that serves its purpose with comfort and everlasting style.

RIGHT
Stylish hardware and visible plumbing add to the tailored, unpretentious attitude of this bathroom. The open-leg-style console contributes to the room's spacious feel, while a band of boldly colored tile breaks the white monochromatic palette, thwarting a sterile, cold appearance.

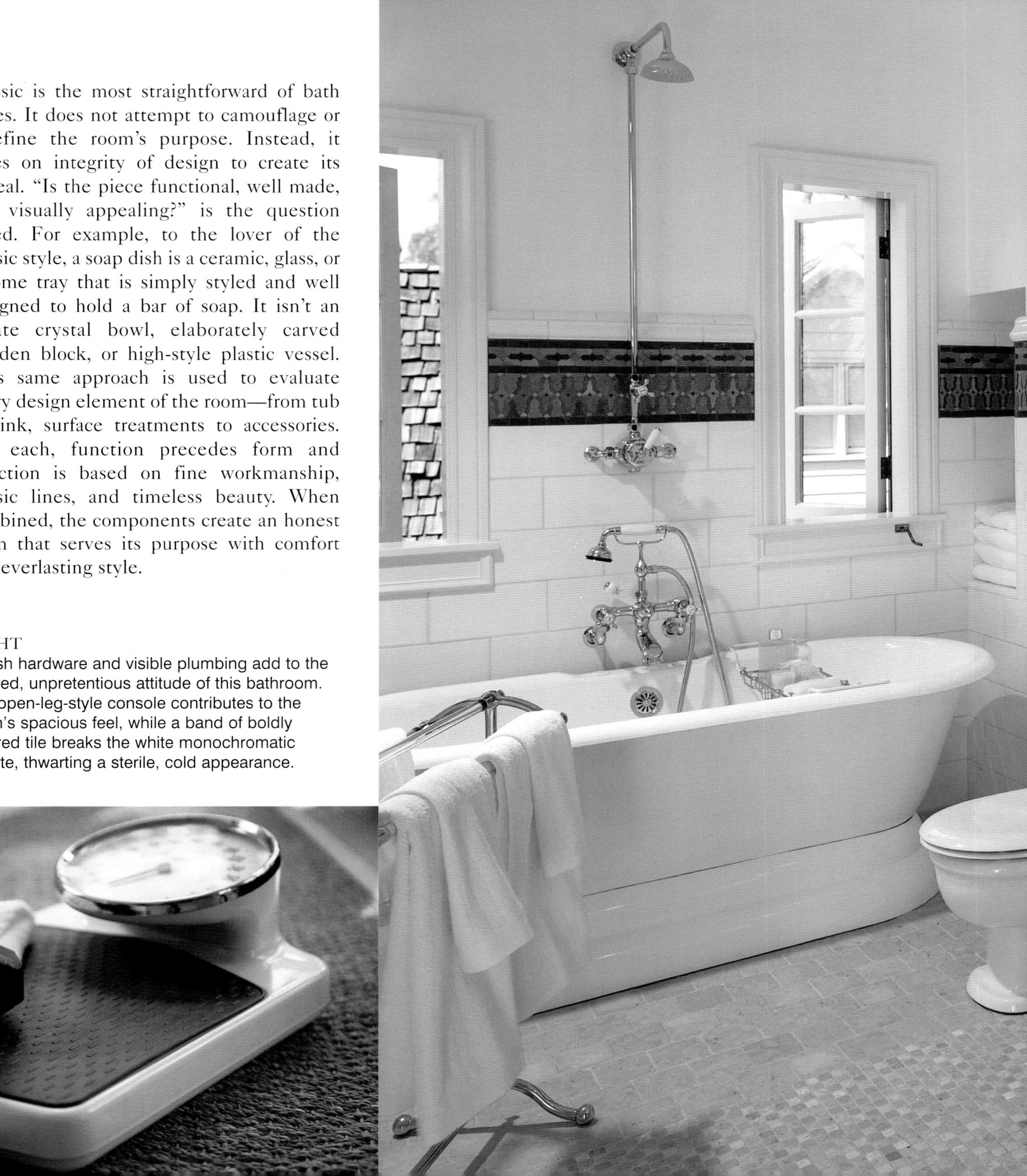

There are many faces to the classic-style bath. While they all share a timeless, unassuming attitude, their forms, fixtures, and finishes can vary greatly. A popular version of this bathroom integrates natural materials and textures. Rather than glossy tile, it dresses in wood paneling or beaded wainscoting. Hardwood and sisal rugs cover the floors while understated skylights and rough-hewn beams float above. Fixtures are kept simple while the silhouettes of the hardware and lighting boast a period style. Accessories are comforting and familiar—photographs, collected rocks, shells, apothecary jars filled with lotions and oils. This bath is like a pair of favorite slippers. It is comforting to slip into and fits just right.

RIGHT
Pure and simple style requires as much attention to detail as does any other look. Here, the white-painted wainscoting and timeless pedestal sink set the perfect stage for carefully selected plumbing, fittings, and coordinated towel rods.

OPPOSITE
The seaside home is an ideal setting for the natural essence of a classic bath. This room's timeless white backdrop wears the wood, stone, and indigenous shapes of shells and starfish with ease and a relaxed beauty.

MODERN STYLE

A passion for gleaming surfaces, fluid lines, and a sophisticated use of materials is at the heart of the modern bathroom. Here, every surface, fixture, and accent is viewed as an opportunity to both add style and visual interest to this streamlined room. Angles and geometric shapes are incorporated to create drama. Brushed steel, chrome, stone, and etched glass are among the leading materials that induce excitement. Walls are subtly detailed and colored as they become the backdrop for state-of-the-art fittings paired with uniquely formed fixtures. Consoles or pedestals replace the traditionally used vanity while unadorned or imaginatively framed mirrors in all shapes and sizes are used as focal points in the room. Accessories are kept to a minimum and are frequently highly stylized versions of the bathroom's necessities. Superfluous objects and clutter are not at home here. The same holds true of elaborate window coverings. Instead, blinds, screens, or unique panels are used to provide privacy. If the look seems too stern, suede, rich fabrics, and imaginative lighting can be used to soften the hard edges. While this style may seem austere to some, its lack of clutter and ornamentation is liberating to others. The appeal of this bath lies in the clarity of its design, the uniqueness of its fabrication, and the performance of its elements. It is clean, dramatic, and undeniably chic.

Created from scratch, the modern bath is a work of art in which every element directly contributes to the style of the room. In preexisting bathrooms, however, established fixtures, surface treatments, and accents can become obstacles in an attempt to develop this striking style. This is where the power of detail steps in. Simple, and often inexpensive changes in detail can be made to help turn a nondescript bathroom into a modern showcase. First, and foremost, excess clutter and decoration must be removed. Fussy shower curtains, window treatments, wall coverings, and towels must be replaced with tailored, understated versions. Abundant accessories, perfume bottles, potpourri bowls, baskets, and decanters should be discarded or hidden away. After all, the intrigue of this look is largely derived from its streamlined, orderly character. Undressed or simply framed mirrors can replace ornately decorated pieces. Black-and-white photography or abstract paintings replace landscapes or watercolors. Glass or stainless-steel accessories effectively relieve plastic, wood, or gilded soap dishes, towel racks, and robe hooks. Even the easy task of changing porcelain or brass hardware to sculpted, brushed-nickel or chrome-plated handles can make a huge difference. Look to every detail in the room, add material interest, and simplify it in texture and form. The result: a bathroom alive with the magnetism of the modern style.

ABOVE AND OPPOSITE
Stainless-steel bowls paired with the severe edges of glass, stone, and concrete create a dramatically modern statement in each of these uniquely and imaginatively fabricated bathrooms.

RIGHT
With few accessories in the room, the modern bath relies upon the forms and finishes of even its most indispensable "tools" to add style. The hairdryer and soap dish are no exceptions.

Simplicity is the ultimate sophistication.

Leonardo da Vinci

Far from spontaneous, the modern-style bath merges form and function with a discerning eye. This doesn't mean the room is empty, cold, or clinical—far from it. With a selective take on the shapes and finishes of the room's limited components, you can create a stunning space that radiates refreshing clarity. These rooms, for example, use warm, dark wood to color the white backdrops with seductive sophistication. Each fixture—undulatory handles at the sink, a halo-like shower rod, tub-side bath/shower mixers—add a sense of sculpture to the spaces. Clean, square edges and the pattern play of tile mosaics and highly grained woods enrich these handsomely detailed bathrooms.

LEFT AND ABOVE
Every item of the modern bath can, and should, contribute to its daring style. From the toothbrush and towel holders, to the shelving and carefully selected objects it displays, each offers a simple and powerful way to add to the room's energy and strength.

OPPOSITE
In the modern bath, where the look can become cool and detached, one must create opportunities to make bold statements of personal style. This collector's racing poster and model car are smartly displayed to accentuate the room's clean lines while adding engaging wit and color.

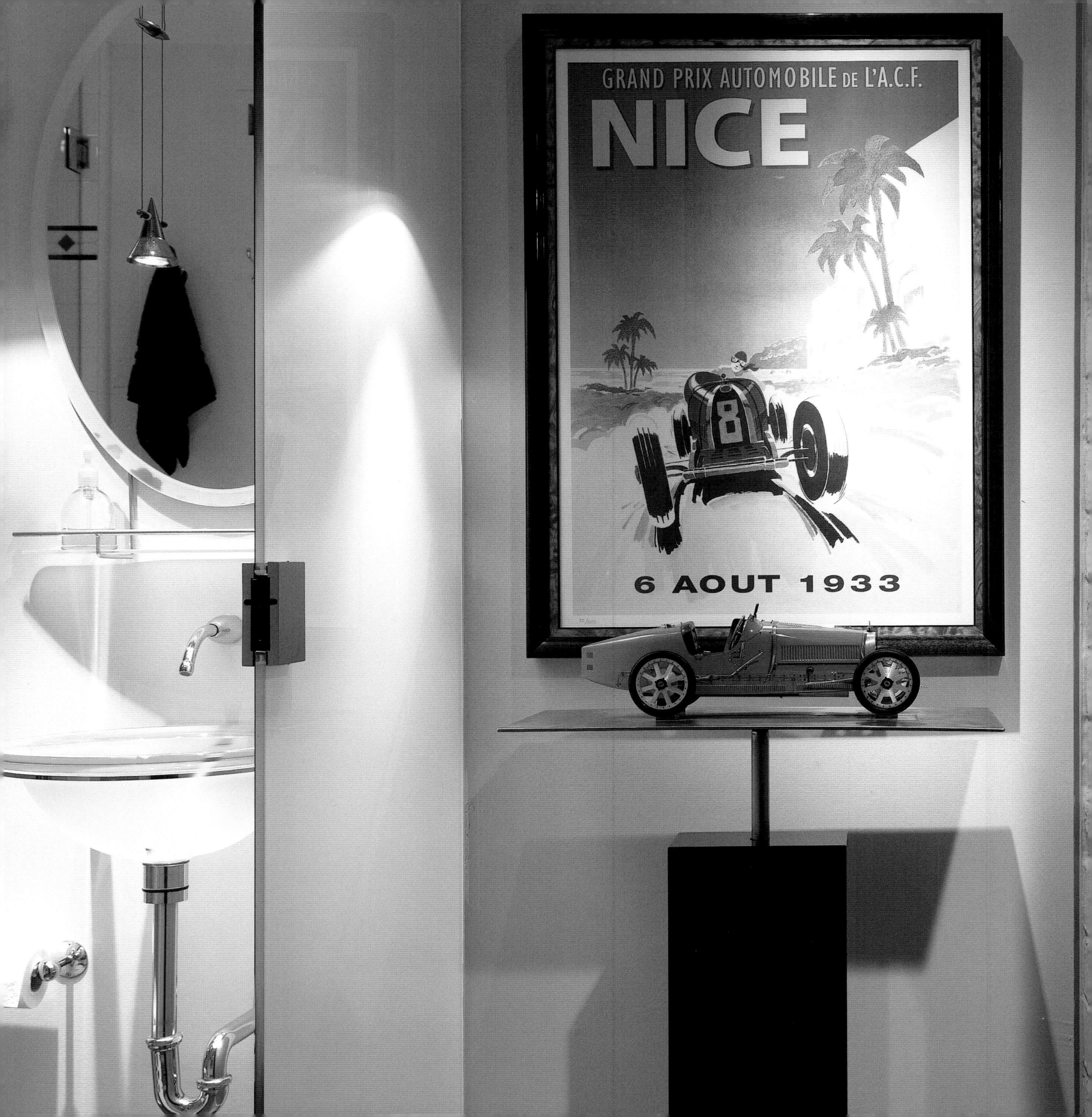
GRAND PRIX AUTOMOBILE DE L'A.C.F.
NICE
8
6 AOUT 1933

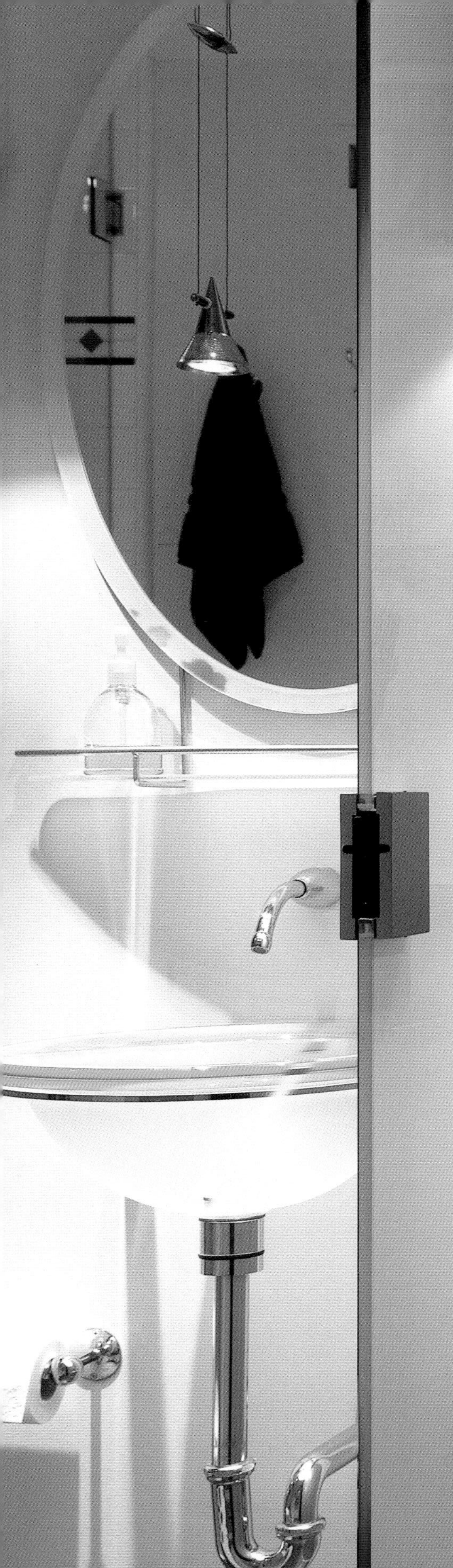

What better room to bring your fantasy style to life than the bathroom? By its very nature, it is a private, personal space that boldly welcomes the imaginative use of detail. Because fantasies are unique to each person, so are fantasy-style baths. One person may dream of a sumptuously rich bathroom with fluted columns and marble floors, while another's idea of paradise may be glamorously chic Art Deco style. The key to creating the fantasy bathroom is to look at every feature and fixture as a way to fulfill your desires. Ask the question "why not?" and set your imagination free. Why not use a stone column rather than a plain wall for support? Why not replace a characterless cabinet with an antique chest or bureau? Why not use an oar as a curtain rod or an enormous shell as a sink bowl? Why not cover a window with a Moroccan screen rather than draperies, or use intricately cut ceramic and

FANTASY STYLE

glass mosaics rather than square tiles in the shower? You get the idea. Set your imagination free. After all, the cookie-cutter bathroom of yesterday has given way to the personalized wants of its occupants; nothing is out-of-bounds. Today, there is no end to the many ways to transform an ordinary bath into an extraordinary shrine that fulfills your one-of-a-kind fantasy.

PAGE 41
Few can dream of a bath that captures the extravagant details of this spectacular room. Fluted stone columns, boldly tiled surfaces, and a pair of richly finished bow-front vanities are just the beginning of the elements that take this room beyond imagination.

RIGHT
Proof that quality wins over quantity, this powder room makes use of its few, but very important, components to create its distinctive look. Foremost, the room's shell—walls, ceiling, and floor—is wondrously set with stone, mosaics, and wood to envelope the bathroom in old-world charm.

OPPOSITE
Even the simplest bathroom can become a fantasy when crowned with fanciful treatments. A metal Moroccan mirror, lording over a mix of hand-forged iron and spice-shaded accents, is at home on the timeworn saffron-colored walls.

Reality can be beaten with enough imagination.

Anonymous

To invent a fantasy-style bath, allow yourself to dream. Look beyond the traditional bathroom setting to find examples of your desired style, then incorporate them into your own bathroom. Import iron gates or a water-spurting fountainhead from the garden. Invite a carved chandelier, lighted candelabra, or wall sconces to illuminate the room. Introduce a tray of smooth stones and a bamboo chaise. Install a vibrant stained-glass window and drape fringed curtains throughout. The creative possibilities are boundless.

OPPOSITE
The brilliance of this bath lies in the illusions it presents. Here, nothing is as it seems. The stainless-steel walls are solid, yet they are broken with stripes of light. The single sculpted faucet becomes doubled when mounted on a mirror and the black granite sink slopes forward as if to spill on the floor.

RIGHT
The bathtub is frequently the focal point of the fantasy-style bath. It is the center of the room, offering itself for luxurious soaks in the seclusion of the dream-inspired room. For this reason, it deserves over-the-top detail. Whether you enclose it with screens, drapes, or columns; cover it with stone, metal, or wood; or accessorize it with candles, fountains, or exotic plants; it becomes the throne of the space. In this striking bathroom, the tub is raised, and faced with a stone step to heighten its importance.

SHELL

Have you ever noticed that the more beautifully a package is wrapped, the more special its contents seem to be? The same holds true of today's bathroom. The more decorative interest lavished upon the shell of the space—walls, floors, ceiling—the more impressive the room looks and the more impact its fixtures, features, and accents appear to have. Surfaces set the decorative tone for the entire room. In fact, more than any other room in the home, the bathroom actually relies on its surfaces to create the ambience of the space. Take away the functional fixtures in the room and the surfaces may be the only large elements open to engaging detail and design. They may be the best way to place one's personal thumbprint of style on the room. Some people prefer understated, minimalistic baths in which the surfaces play the leading role; while others may like heavily adorned rooms brimming over with accessories, fabrics, furnishings, and elaborate finishes. In either case, the atmosphere of the room begins with its shell.

Clearly the bathroom has practical requirements for its surfaces. Considering the steam, splashing water, and endless squirts, splatterings, and bloops of cosmetics, lotions, and pastes, the selection of surfaces must be given careful thought. Maintenance, durability, hygiene, and comfort must be added to aesthetics when determining the perfect surface materials and treatments for your bath. This doesn't mean that only one surface treatment can be used. Some rooms have zones where their exposure to elements change. Tile or stone can be used by the tub and shower, while carpeting, fabric, and delicate finishes adorn the dressing and lounge area of the room. The key is to think outside of the box and embrace uniquely detailed surfaces that amplify the mood of your personal retreat.

If your walls could talk, what would they say? Figuratively, they do talk—they speak of the character and personality of your home. In the bath, the walls welcome design and detail that range from cutting edge to timeless.

WALLS

They may be inspirited by other lands, nature's wonders, or pure imagination. What inspires you? Is it the sparkling waters of the Aegean Sea or the iridescent mosaics of a Turkish Mosque? Maybe it is the serenity of a Zen garden or the traditionalism of an antebellum mansion. Whatever shapes your choice, the walls are open to your interpretation. They can be adorned with any number of materials. Some practical, others nearly inconceivable. Some are used solo, while others are paired and partnered. Of all the choices, tile is the most popular. Others include marble, wood paneling, plaster, paper, stone, and, of course, simple paint. For the more daring, glass block, wall-to-wall mirrors, stainless steel, bamboo, or teak are possibilities. Whatever the decorative direction taken, today's successfully detailed bath wears walls that weather the functional demands of the room while, at the same time, dress to tell of your unique and personal style.

Well-chosen wall surfaces combine form with function in today's bathroom. This shouldn't limit your creativity, though, as there are many materials that can stand up to the adverse elements of water and steam common to most baths. They can perform perfectly and still provide head-turning style. Also, keep in mind that each bath, as well as each part of its space, may make distinct, practical demands that can be addressed by any number of materials. For example, for the wet areas of the bath, tile, glass block, stone, and even treated wood are viable ways to dress the walls.

For areas beyond the threat of soaking and splashing, the sky is the limit. The lavatory, dressing, and passage areas of the room offer countless design-oriented opportunities. From beaded-wood paneling to Venetian plaster, rugged stone to stunning faux finishes, nearly anything can be used to create a striking statement. Also, mounted details—art, mirrors, shelving, rods, hooks—add to the wall's flavor. The key to successfully detailing bathroom walls is to satisfy the working requirements of the space while exploiting the surface's decorative potential in every way possible.

PAGE 47
A jagged-edged ceiling sculpted of drywall, Styrofoam®, and mud is wondrously suspended over, and paired with, faux-finished walls partially faced with broken-edged travertine.

PAGE 49
In this extraordinary bathroom, the walls submerge you in richly toned images of fish and murky waters. Every fixture is exploited to add to the decorative effect. Even the custom towel holder is tooled to look like a current-swept marine plant.

OPPOSITE LOWER LEFT
Never underestimate the power of texture. It can turn an unremarkable surface into a study of light and shadow. The walls of this room are heavily striated and highlighted with a metallic finish. They contrast brilliantly with the polished surfaces of the vanity and hardware.

OPPOSITE UPPER RIGHT
Reflecting the simply finished back walls of this bath, a large horizontal mirror bisects a texture-rich wall of heavily woven cable. These three diverse surface treatments work in harmony to give the space a clean yet fascinating look.

RIGHT
The reflective properties of a wall finish can visually alter the perception of a room's space. Here, the spectacular burnished gold finish of this room's walls enrich it dramatically while appearing to deepen its area. Small raised scroll motifs frame the area around the vanity like pieces of hand-tooled jewelry. For further detailing, the mirror is cleverly suspended by gold chain, rather than being simply mounted on the wall.

RIGHT
One visit to this fascinating bath is not enough to take in all the wondrous images that detail its walls. What is real and what is not? Is the ceiling really draped with luxurious fabric and the ornate mirror framed by dangling tassels? Has a living crow mischievously knocked a china vase off the window-sill, leaving it broken in shards on the floor below? Is some or all of the shattered vase real? And what about the window? Is it a simulated scene of open sky or an actual iron grate that invites the outdoors in? Thanks to this brilliantly adorned room, answers to these questions require a closer inspection of its surfaces—the art that is its walls.

I don't want realism. I want magic.

Tennessee Williams

To some, the urge to turn an everyday bath into a parade of surprising details is irresistible. On the walls, one of the most evocative treatments is trompe l'oeil. Literally meaning "to fool the eye," trompe l'oeil uses painted imagery to create extraordinary effects that transform a flat surface into a three-dimensional slice of life. This treatment adds depth and drama to baths of many styles. It can create the impression of interesting architecture, invite life-like scenery, and lavish fanciful objects upon a room. Well-executed trompe l'oeil delights the onlooker and often requires a touch test to determine whether a detail is real or the result of an extraordinary slight of hand.

Its elemental beauty and expressive character have made stone one of the top choices for surfacing in today's bath. From richly polished marble to softly honed limestone and rugged flagstone, this age-old material can bring an unmatched strength, both structurally and decoratively, to the room. Floors, countertops, sinks, and tubs, all open themselves to stone's imposing personality. So do the walls. Stone adds texture, color, and an ageless permanence to this surface and pairs harmoniously with wood, metal, ceramic, and glass. It can be used in large square tiles, irregular slabs, sharp-edged shards, intricate mosaics, and even smooth pebbles. Regardless of its form, stone flatters most any style bathroom with its many looks—sleek, classic, rustic, opulent, organic, and even understated. Like no other material, it can impose a timeless and natural beauty to almost every surface it touches.

RIGHT
Like any material used in excess, stone can overwhelm a bathroom. By selectively using the stone on side and accent walls, this bath exploits its rugged texture and irregular pattern to perfectly frame the more refined vanity and polished-stone countertop.

OPPOSITE
As if set into an outcropping of rugged rock, this tub looks out upon a view of beautifully vegetated desert. The jagged stone slabs that climb the tub's otherwise unadorned walls repeat the natural, open look of the home's native landscape. The assorted sizes and shapes of fragments that face the tub's step add interest and character.

One of the most important criteria for a bathroom floor is practicality. But that doesn't mean it must be cold or stark. Today, the bath enjoys a high status in the home and with this has come a selection of flooring that was once considered for only the most visible and public rooms of the house. Plush carpeting, elegant marble, natural stone, and varnished wood accompany tile, vinyl, and linoleum as wonderful options for the bathroom's flooring. Each has its advantages and disadvantages, depending on how the room will be used, who will be using it, and in which area of the bath it is placed. Once these are determined, the floodgate of choices opens. Include in your decision process not only what material will be used but how you can make the most of it to bring a one-of-a-kind look to your bath. Carpet can be surrounded with a

FLOORS

marble border, tile can be set on the diagonal and used in assorted colors, and wood can be painted, used in various widths, or paired with other materials. Of course, area rugs, luxurious bath mats, and varnished hand-painted canvases can be used to cover and accent any underlying surface. The possibilities are infinite. Bear in mind that while the floor of the bathroom has a functional job to do, its color, pattern, and texture lay the groundwork for the room's overall style.

The flooring of the bath plays to your senses every time you enter the room. Walk into your bathroom and experience the floor visually. Its color, pattern, and sheen can calm, excite, or intrigue you. Now close your eyes. How does the floor feel? Do you savor the cushioning of plush carpeting, the coolness of tile and stone, or the slight give of natural wood? Now listen. Every flooring surface also has its own sound—rugs and carpeting are muted, sisal crunches, and wood can creak. Clearly, the surface of the bathroom floor is alive with personality.

PAGE 57
Large stone tiles are inset into the center of this bathroom's stone floor to create the illusion of a bold and beautiful area rug. It adds immeasurable character while visually breaking up the area and helping to define the room's space.

RIGHT
Sometimes the floor is the backdrop to a room's style and other times it actually creates it. Here, antique European hand-painted tiles become the focal point of this small bath, defining its character. As the flooring for a historic home, this timeworn tile is perfect.

OPPOSITE LOWER LEFT
A simple checkerboard grid of tile unifies this handsome bathroom. In larger tiles, it dresses the floor while the walls boast a smaller version of the same pattern. By setting the grid square rather than diagonal in the room, the treatment gives the room a clean, modern look.

OPPOSITE UPPER RIGHT
An undulating pattern of mosaic tiles sets the tone of this bathroom's floor. The small rhythmic pattern and bordering plain white tile defines the space while balancing the larger brick-layer pattern on the walls.

OPPOSITE LOWER RIGHT
Never underestimate the power of a great rug. This arrestingly patterned kilim directs the style and color of this otherwise monochromatic bath. A simple switch to a different rug and the look and feel of the room would change entirely.

Pattern is one of the floor's most important vehicles of style. It works with color, shape, and texture to bring rhythm and design to an otherwise plain and motionless ground. It may naturally exist in materials (like veining in marble) or be the result of artistic expression (like hand-painted ceramics). Often, it results from the orchestrated placement of identical or mixed materials. Randomly laid flagstone or a latticework design of wood and stone are examples of patterned arrangements. Sometimes space between the integrated materials of a floor produce its visual punch. For instance, the strength of a ceramic tile grid becomes greater with a wide grout line of a contrasting color. The pattern becomes a bold geometric design. Narrow, discreet grout lines will tame a tile floor's design. Simply determine the vitality and personality desired of your floor and consider the use of pattern to deliver the look you want.

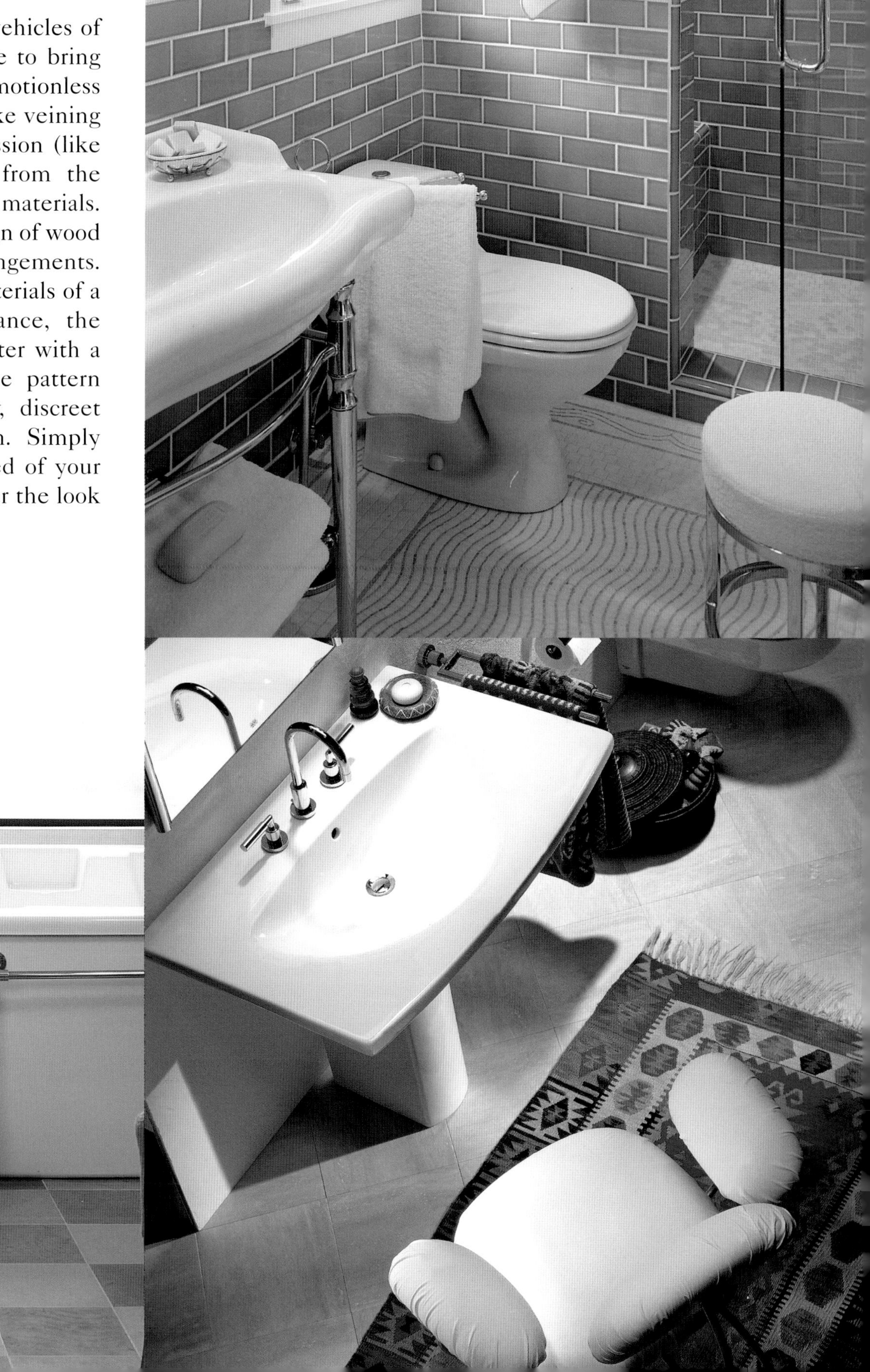

The walls and floors of the bath team up to create the backdrop of the room. By uniting them with decorative detail, you can double the effect each has on the character of the space. One way to accomplish this is by using identical or similar materials on both surfaces. Tile or wood on the floor, for example, can continue up the wall or be featured somewhere on its face. Another method of tying the two together is to repeat the pattern of one surface on the other. This works even if they utilize different materials. For instance, a running stone border in the floor can be copied in paint and stenciled at the top of the wall. The same pattern can be etched on a glass screen or carved on wood trim. Finally, merge the floor and wall with common colors or textures. The rich hue from the green marble floor could color the glass mosaic trim around the vanity or the paint on the walls.

LEFT
On a Rorschach test, these free-form colored blobs may have some hidden meaning, but in this bath they are purely for fun. They are proof that even the simplest detail can add enormous character to a space and that by using it on both the walls and the floor, it makes twice the impression on all who see it.

RIGHT
Spacious bathrooms are perfect for large surface patterns. Small and intricate designs can get lost and seem inappropriate here. In this roomy master suite, a geometric play of pattern and color flourishes on its surfaces. A bordered stone “area rug” centers the room and spawns coordinating designs on the trim and expansive planes of the walls.

What's the view you see when lying in your bathtub? If it is a plain white ceiling, it may be time to let detail bring this overhead surface to life. While the ceiling may not have to work

CEILINGS

as diligently as the bath's walls and the floor, it can contribute significantly to the room's personality. What's more, the ceiling surface has little to obstruct your creativity. Aside from lighting fixtures or overhead fans, which are details themselves, the ceiling is a blank canvas inviting your creative treatments. Let your imagination roam. Of course, the simplest treatment is color. It can enliven the surface and visually alter its height. The more intense or dark the color, the more it appears to lower the ceiling. The reverse is true of lighter shades. A stenciled border on the ceiling or adjoining wall will draw the eye upward. Architectural moldings, cornices, and beams do the same. Wallpaper, fabric, plaster reliefs, and paneling are other options. Clever use of trompe l'oeil can open the ceiling to images of star-filled skies, a canopy of leafy branches, or a mural of the sun and clouds. And don't overlook lighting. Skylights and distinctive fixtures can add pizzazz to a plain ceiling as can the shadows and spots of light created by sconces and uplights below.

Because the ceiling is overlooked decoratively in most bathrooms, applying an imaginative treatment to yours can set it apart stylistically while adding enormous character to the space. Sometimes bathrooms are blessed with interesting architectural ceiling features. Beams, skylights, coving, and pitched surfaces, all lend overhead interest. By applying color, textural interest, or pattern to these, you can exaggerate their decorative influence on the room. Plainer ceilings may not be as interesting as those with architectural interest, but they are often simpler to detail and the impact can be as spectacular. From fabric draped like the peak of a tent to sparkling stars on a dark blue background, the decorative options for the ceiling are limited only by your imagination. Aim high in your endeavors.

UPPER LEFT
A simple antique-gold finish on the ceiling adds to the richness and elegance of this beautiful powder room. The gilded mirror and high-style art tie the finish to the rest of the room.

RIGHT
In a natural Zen-like bath, a wooden grid acts as an overhead screen to fill the space with softly diffused light. It also brings the lofty ceiling down to a level that makes the room more intimate and comfortable.

OPPOSITE
A patchwork of woven-rug swatches crowns this distinctively styled bath. By enlisting a material more commonly used on the floor, this spectacular ceiling becomes proof of the power of imaginative detailing.

FIXTURES

Whether your bathroom is a resort-like refuge, a stunning contemporary creation, or a timelessly traditional space, it will contain elements common to all bathrooms—the sink, bathtub, shower, toilet, and bidet. Not every bathroom has each one of these elements; but odds are, it has a majority of them. They are the workers of the room. They must operate and function efficiently in order for the room to be enjoyable. Besides their practical performance, they can also help drive the direction of the room's look and feel. Their forms, colors, and finishes, all influence the style of the bathroom. For example, a ball & claw-footed tub and a pedestal sink are the foundation of a period look. A tub, shower, and basin clad in stainless steel ensure a bathroom's modern edge. The list goes on. As the fixtures of the bath have literally become its furnishings, the manufacturers of these pieces have become artisans who have turned these everyday "necessities" into brilliant art forms. There are sinks that appear to float in midair, bathtubs of endless shapes, and walk-in showers that double as steam rooms and have jets that spray from every direction. Even an older bath, sink, or shower clad with basic fittings can be brought to life with the addition of a new sculptured faucet, chiseled handles, or scrolled towel bars. Like jewelry that transforms a simple dress from ordinary to extraordinary, hardware can turn even the most basic fixtures of the bath into something special.

Ease into its embrace. Close your eyes and relish the soft, silky water that engulfs you. Feel its smooth surface and inhale the aroma of herbal soaps and oils. Listen to the soft splash of water against the silence of

BATH

the room. To many, this is the allure of bathing. It is an experience. And at its core is the bathtub. In both form and function, it is the essence of the many bathrooms. The bathtub comes in many shapes and sizes, materials and colors. It can fit discreetly in the corner of the room or take center stage in the middle of the space. Its silhouette and fabrication can suggest a style of centuries past or speak of contemporary milieus. It can be starkly presented among beautiful views or surrounded by rich stone, bold tiles, brilliant mosaics, and drapes of luxurious fabrics. Furnished with indulgent bath salts, loofahs, and thick thirsty towels, it can irresistibly tempt one to a long and blissful soak. To the unenlightened, the bathtub may be just another fixture. To others, however, it is a way to stylistically set the tone of their dream bathroom while creating an irresistible place to wash away the toils and trials of the day.

What does your bathtub say about you? Is it discreetly positioned out of the way and staged for a quick dip? Or, on the other hand, is it regally placed in the room, highly stylized, and equipped with all of the amenities needed for long, indulgent soaks? Does it "fit" as you slide into its form? Does it allow you to stretch out and fully submerge yourself in the soothing water? And how does it look? Is it appropriate to the size and shape of the room? Does it stylistically help create the look and feel you desire?

Some uniquely designed tubs—copper, marble, and antique ball & claw for example, need little assistance to make a statement. They can stand on their own aesthetically. The more-standard acrylic or cast-iron models, however, often require a little help. To add character to the basic fixture, you must view it as an experience. What would make it more exciting to see and enticing to use? A tub can float under a ceiling of painted scenes, a striped fabric awning, or an elegant chandelier. It can be dressed with an apron of marble, tile, or tongue-and-groove wood from its rim to the floor. It can be framed or shrouded in luxurious textiles. Exotic screens can surround it, providing privacy and character. Small nearby tables, boxes, and stands can be staged to provide a place to display anything from candles and lotions to a small lamp and a favorite book. Head-turning hardware can replace more-basic issue. And the accessories—caddies that span the tub's width, oils, sponges, stylish hooks and bars, luscious towels, textured floor mats—are all ways to turn a nondescript tub into an experience that seduces you to linger every time you enter the room.

LEFT
In contemporary to traditionally styled bathrooms, the tub can serve as the core of the room's experience, spacially and decoratively.

OPPOSITE
Capitalizing on the fluid form of this beautiful bath, hand-painted scroll designs adorn its sides. They exude an elegance and style that turns this room into a restful retreat.

Give your bath a sensual treat. Splurge on accoutrements that delight the eye and pamper your senses. Turn even the most modest bathroom into a hedonistic retreat. Sparkling glass bottles and stone jars filled with soothing oils, perfumed salts, and milky lotions bathe the room in luxury. Loofahs, sponges, and brushes rub and exfoliate while plush, thirsty towels softly dry. This is the essence of pure indulgence.

Give me the luxuries of life and I will willingly do without the necessities.

Frank Lloyd Wright

Opening the bathroom to the outdoors can add a new dimension to the room. Whether it is through a wall of glass overlooking a lush garden or an open French door that steps out onto a private patio, the view will expand both the character and perceptual space of the room. Windows virtually tie the bath to the landscape decoratively, bringing the colors, textures, and forms of the outdoors in. This, in turn, increases the design and decorative options for the interior space. Many beautiful bathrooms actually draw upon the nature of the landscape and utilize it in their design schemes. For example, a vista of palms becomes the impetus for a tropical or Oriental theme. Rugged mountains or open deserts suggest the use of raw stone and rugged hardware. In fact, indigenous materials taken from the land can be extremely effective when used directly in the space. Flagstone floors, knotty-pine cabinets, bamboo walls, and even seashell-embedded tile are examples of inspired design elements derived from the neighboring landscape.

PAGE 72
Exquisitely handcrafted from copper, this shapely tub lures bathers with its deep form and distinctive style. A mix of stone covered surfaces and a towel-laden ladder complete this bathroom's ambience perfectly.

UPPER RIGHT
Seen from the hallway, the French doors of this bathroom lure one into the room. The tub is perfectly positioned to take advantage of the view outside.

LOWER RIGHT
By opening this bath to a charming patio, the designer has expanded the space of the richly appointed room while providing a perfect place to wash up when coming in from out of doors.

OPPOSITE
Overlooking a beautiful private patio, this bath is an oasis encased in smooth stone and panes of glass. The restrained use of pattern and texture inside allows bathers to concentrate on the delightful view outdoors.

HARDWARE

Hardware was once unappreciated, overlooked, and haphazardly chosen. Today, it is experiencing a renaissance of sorts and has achieved the status of an art form. For the tub alone, the wealth of options is impressive. Faucets, handles, valves, and drains direct the water while they punctuate the decorative statement of the room. Like jewelry, hardware accessorizes the tub with a specific style. Also like jewelry, it is fashioned in an assortment of shapes, forms, finishes, and colors. By carefully considering the style of your room when you select your bath's hardware, the result can be spectacular.

OPPOSITE UPPER LEFT
This elegant matte-finished hardware features a retractable handset that discreetly stores within the tub surround for a clean, uncluttered look.

OPPOSITE LOWER LEFT
A modern take on the classic bath/shower mixer, this piece uses a shiny chrome finish and tubular forms to update the age-old silhouette and crosshead handles of the fixture.

OPPOSITE UPPER RIGHT
A traditional telephone handset perfectly accents the classic-style bath while providing flexibility and range of motion for thoroughly rinsing the body as well as the tub itself.

OPPOSITE LOWER RIGHT
Because this softly curved gooseneck faucet is placed at the tub's center, there is no obstruction for a bather while resting his or her head at either end of the bath.

While the bath is meant for us to relax, the shower is created to revitalize and invigorate. Free-flowing, pulsating, and massaging streams of water have turned the five-minute wash-and-rinse shower of yesterday into an extended exhilarating experience, limited only by the supply of hot water available. What has also changed with

SHOWER

today's shower is its look, size, and shape. Imaginative design and decorative details are lavished on the shower, making its appearance as stimulating as the water-spraying fittings mounted inside. Structurally, the shower is open to bold strokes of creativity. The tired look of a plastic curtain hanging from a rod has given way to walls of glass block, smooth stone, curvaceous plaster, vibrant tile, and panes of frosted and etched glass. Luxurious fabrics, backed with liners, can also be used to frame and flatter the fixture. Simply stated, if a surface is waterproof, it is a viable option for enclosing the shower. To decoratively tie the shower to the rest of the bathroom, it can borrow treatments from other surfaces in the room. Bordered floor tiles may climb up the shower's walls and the marble or honed stone used on countertops may face or outline the shower's enclosure. Mosaics and distinctive hardware used elsewhere are additional ways to decoratively marry the shower to the rest of the space. The options are infinite. While there may always be the debate about the personal preference of the shower versus the tub, there can be no argument about the strength of today's shower as a way to bring unbounded style to the room.

The shower is like a room within the bathroom itself. And just like the larger space, it can be dressed with unique and eye-catching detail. Through imaginative design, the shower can be a continuation of the surrounding space by incorporating the surface treatments lavished upon the larger space. Elaborately laid tile, stone, and decorative glass can flow from the bathroom into the shower enclosure, highlighting the walls, floor, and even the ceiling. On the other hand, the shower can become a world of its own, enriched with materials and treatments unique to it alone. Rugged rock, hand-painted tile, brushed steel, and beautiful fabric treatments, all offer decorative potential as they surround the shower with its own distinctive character.

PAGE 79
Recognizing the luxury of open floor space, this bath uses glass walls on this majestic, centrally positioned shower to accommodate it in the room. Monochromatic stone and a liberal use of mirrors throughout help to accentuate this master bath's spaciousness.

ABOVE AND RIGHT
What was once a blight on the well-decorated bathroom, the shower curtain has been reborn with beautiful materials, colors, and patterns. Even the simplest curtains become assets of the bath, incorporating stylish rods and rings.

There was a time when the box-like stall or curtained tub defined the typical shower. Today, this fixture can be tailor-made to specifically fit the size, shape, and style of your bath. Corner, circular, and angular shower "pods" graciously suffice in constrained, tight bathrooms. While they are small in size, their stylized surrounds and hardware make them big in personality. For today's more spacious bathrooms, elaborately designed walk-in showers have become the rage. Designed to accommodate more than one bather, they are extravagantly appointed with rich surfaces, benches, and specialized fittings that spray, soak, steam, and massage their pampered occupants.

LEFT
A curved wall of translucent-glass block juxtaposed with jagged flagstone creates a striking architectural enclosure for this shower. The materials add pure theatre to the room while drawing light into the shower space.

Why settle for a plastic curtain or an unadorned sheet of glass when you can incorporate distinctively detailed shower surrounds to bring drama and character to your bathroom? Architectural and art-like enclosures of chiseled, frosted, crackled, or stenciled glass can replace everyday metal-framed panes to create a spectacular focal point for the room. The surround can repeat forms and finishes found elsewhere in the room to punctuate a distinctive look or theme. Further, the shape and opening of the enclosure can be dramatically detailed by incorporating eye-catching doors and screens that uniquely pivot, fold, or slide.

UPPER LEFT
Bevel-edged panes of glass are bracketed together with matte aluminum joints to encase this highly stylized shower. Multiple body sprays, a water-fountain spout, sandblasted windows, and a built-in bench are among the feature's amenities. The broken-edged flooring tiles add dramatic detail while creating a nonslip surface.

LOWER RIGHT
This walk-in shower features a glass enclosure magnificently detailed to mimic the silhouettes of the mountainous landscape. Inside, it is equipped with a bench, windows, and multiple showerheads including a ceiling-mounted rain-shower fixture.

OPPOSITE
Finished to replicate an eroded slab of stone, the glass enclosure of this step-in shower elevates this simple fixture into a sculpted work of art.

Few things are as invigorating and refreshing as an outdoor shower. Feeling a stream of water pour down while fresh air and sunlight surround you is pure bliss. Today, some imaginatively designed baths have ventured outdoors by placing a secondary shower just outside of the interior space. This feature provides a fair-weather option for everyday cleansing as well as a place to rinse after toiling in the yard or enjoying a day at the pool or the beach. Decoratively, surface treatments and distinctive materials used inside are often shared with the outdoor fixture. Colorful tile, flagstone, oiled wood, and sparkling glass block are just a few of the options that are practical in both interior and exterior spaces. These, and other materials can visually tie the shower to the adjacent bath while giving it color and character of its own. A word of advice: If you decoratively connect the outdoor shower to the indoor space, make certain that the materials and details used are able to withstand the outdoor elements and are also complementary to the exterior style of the home.

PAGE 84
A curved wall of glass block decoratively encompasses this outdoor shower, while a motif of sandblasted tropical leaves on the shower door provides detail and the illusion of privacy.

PAGE 85
Sometimes outdoor showers can leave you feeling exposed. Here, the fixture is enclosed while still allowing you to commune with nature. An overhead grid of pine vegas, a curved wall with open "windows," and an interior treatment of rugged stone combine to create a private yet open shower.

RIGHT
Who said showers are boring? This innovative shower system takes everyday cleansing to new heights. The tower can be installed with a single plumbing connection and boasts multiple water ports that can be adjusted in direction and height to customize the fixture.

OPPOSITE UPPER RIGHT
This modern bathroom features an inventive shower system that indulges its occupant with a waterfall spout and rows of stimulating water jets. A slide-out seat provides a place to sit while taking in all the pleasures the shower unit has to offer.

OPPOSITE LOWER RIGHT
Floor-to-ceiling travertine tile becomes the perfect backdrop for beautifully designed sliding shower doors. A handsome hand shower and numerous water ports enhance the wash-and-rinse experience of the fixture.

OPPOSITE LOWER LEFT
A perfect fit, this corner fixture has a built-in seat and multiple water ports to house a magnificent shower in a confined space.

Today's shower fittings and hardware are available in an assortment of stunning forms and finishes. Many can turn the brief wash-and-rinse routine into a lingering hydro-therapeutic experience. What appeals to you? Is it the gentle spray of an oversized showerhead or the classic looks and versatility of a continental-style hand-held sprayer? Maybe it is an elaborate set of water jets aimed to massage from all directions. With today's fittings, water does more than cleanse. It relaxes, recharges, and revitalizes through the use of an assortment of innovative fittings. They are used to spray, propel, and rush water to soothe and knead the body. In addition, thermostatic controls can maintain constant water temperature and steam can be infused into enclosed shower stalls, creating a real in-home steam room.

Once upon a time, sinks were viewed as functional, nondescript basins that caught and drained water flowing from humdrum faucets. Not so anymore. Today, sinks and their fittings have become headliners in many of the most spectacularly designed bathrooms. The curvaceous forms, surprising materials, and

SINKS

stunning designs of the sink strongly color the tone of the bath. A clear glass bowl floating above a plate of glass, a hammered-copper basin ensconced in a countertop of antique tile, and a pedestal sink of hand-carved stone, all make a powerful decorative statement. In today's bathroom, sinks are used solo or showcased in pairs. They can be set in an antique chest, supported by an ornate console, or simply mounted on the wall. Each distinct style and display unmistakably influences the room's personality. Whatever your tastes—simply contemporary, richly traditional, daringly dramatic—today's brilliantly fashioned sinks are guaranteed to "bowl" you over!

When most people speak of sinks, they typically refer to what is really the lavatory. A lavatory is the fixture comprised of the bowl, faucet, and stand. In one form or another, it is common to all bathrooms and is one of the most important design elements and details of the room. In fact, in most baths it is the room's primary focal point. Today's lavatories take many forms, from wall-mounted basins and platforms to freestanding pedestals, open consoles, and stylish cabinets and vanities. The basin, or bowl, comes in an assortment of shapes and an array of surprising materials. The crowning touch—the hardware—boasts limitless style and finish options. The old concept of the lavatory has disappeared. We now indulge in ingenious and imaginative silhouettes and materials that open the bath to breathtaking style.

The proper selection of the lavatory depends on a number of practical considerations. What size of lavatory can the bathroom accommodate? Can it house a double sink and a large cabinet or is a space-conscious wall-mounted basin or pedestal sink a better choice? How will it be used? Do you need abundant countertop and storage space that a vanity or cabinet can provide or is a small console adequate? Whom will it serve? The lavatory's height should comfortably suit those who use it. Today, taller vanities and raised basins have become popular as the average person's height has increased since the advent of the 31"-high vintage units. Lavatories up to 36" high are quite common today. What will the fixture be exposed to? The selected material and fabrication of the lavatory should readily stand up to the pastes and creams, lotions and potions common to most bathrooms. In master and family baths, this is very important. In lightly used powder rooms, it is less so.

UPPER RIGHT
A carved-stone trough becomes the headliner sink of this simply styled, yet richly fabricated bathroom. The full-width mirror accentuates the impressive size and character of this unique fixture.

PAGE 89
Like a bowl lined with jewels, this natural geode sparkles beneath hand-tooled hardware to become the one-of-a-kind sink of this stunning bath. The fixture's textural strength is underscored by the room's chiseled-stone walls and countertop edges.

OPPOSITE
Designs-a-plenty make the pedestal a perfect fit for all bath styles. A classically styled porcelain bowl generously serves two (upper left), a carved canterra-stone pedestal resembles an antique Mexican fountain base (upper right), and a sculpted travertine fixture presents a boldly contemporary, southwestern design.

PEDESTAL

The pedestal sink is a study of style and size. From vintage to retro, contemporary to over-the-top silhouettes, the pedestal sink can color the character of any bathroom. It is a natural in a powder room or small bath where space is at a premium and where the room's personality relies on the style of a few powerfully detailed fixtures. While it is not strong on storage, the pedestal does hide plumbing. Its solitary form and unique materials give it an almost sculptural presence that is perfect for the dramatically fashioned bathroom.

CONSOLE

The console is a chic lavatory table that is affixed to the wall and supported by front legs. It can be found or fashioned in limitless styles, fitting for the most contemporary and traditionally styled bathrooms alike. Although it may be short on storage space, its tabletop provides plenty of surface area. Unlike a chest or vanity, the console's open-leg styling lends the bathroom a spacious, airy look. Many consoles are created with rods or lower shelves to hold towels and a small number of bath necessities.

ABOVE
Curvaceous layered metals and a chiseled-edge countertop turn this unique traditional console into a magnificent sculpture.

RIGHT
A broad square bowl and tapered leather-wrapped legs give this classic console a flawlessly tailored look.

OPPOSITE
An armature of curves captured by this brilliant glass bowl and scrolled-iron support make this space-saving fixture a modern masterpiece (upper left). Smooth contours of a white porcelain sink and matching shroud hide the plumbing and provide a bowl for this spare, but stylish bath (lower left). The decorative force of a boxy wall-mounted lavatory flatters the fresh linear design of this fashionable bath (lower right).

WALL MOUNTED

Small in stature but big on style, the wall-mounted sink is the perfect solution for spatially challenged, yet fashion-conscious bathrooms. It can be hung to accommodate the height of any user and leaves the floor space below open and airy. Some hide the sink's plumbing while others boldly display highly polished or vintage pipework. The wall-mounted sink provides no storage for the bath but more than makes up for this with the ingenious silhouettes and materials it offers the room.

BOWLS

Nothing says that a bathroom sink should always be white porcelain. While this may be the perfect choice for some spaces, decorating with basins boasting unusual materials and distinctive finishes has added a whole new dimension to today's high-style bath. Clear glass and polished stainless-steel bowls are a spectacle in a boldly contemporary room. Polished-brass, hammered-copper, and even treated-wood sinks are equally stunning and perfect for rustic and eclectically decorated spaces. Thanks to today's manufacturers, there is an impressive selection of bowls, vessels, and basins available in a broad range of colors, designs, materials, and finishes. But don't stop there. In your search for the perfect sink, let your imagination fly. As the sinks throughout these pages prove, a little gumption and a lot of ingenuity will reward you with a brilliant one-of-a-kind bathroom.

ABOVE AND RIGHT
Created to fit into an existing surface, this rectangular sink appears to be simply sitting on top of this antique pine chest (upper left). A beautiful design in cobalt blue on white graces the bowl, hardware, tile, and even accessories of this unforgettable lavatory (lower left). Astonishing design takes form in this underlit glass bowl and iron-framed onyx console (lower right).

OPPOSITE
A love of the primitive Southwest inspired every decision and detail of this wonderfully decorated bath. The room's focal point, a hammered metal bowl, is the crowning glory of the room's texture-rich character.

*Things are pretty, graceful, rich,
elegant, handsome,
but until they speak to the
imagination, not yet beautiful.*

Ralph Waldo Emerson

There is reason that bath hardware has become one of the most important details in the room. Single-handedly, it can define the decorative style of the bathroom while bringing even the plainest fixture to life. Today's faucets include taps and spouts of every design and finish. They can be mounted on the deck of the sink or on the wall behind it. There can be separate taps that dispense hot and cold water independently or, more commonly, mix the waters to the desired temperature. They can work with single or double handles and flow from spouts of every imaginable shape and silhouette.

When selecting the hardware for a new sink or to replace that of an existing fixture, strongly consider the decorative impact the fittings can make. The scale of the piece, its silhouette, and its finish, all affect its impact. For a classic or traditional bath, porcelain, cross, or six-pronged handles are very fitting. In many minimalist baths, the simpler the hardware, the better. Sculpted spheres, blocks, and swirled handles are more appropriate for eclectic and boldly contemporary rooms. Remember, too, that the finish of the hardware is as important, if not more so, than its shape or silhouette. Shiny chrome, smooth steel, brushed nickel, and copper aged with a time-worn patina, for example, each powerfully yet differently influence the room's statement of style.

EXTRAS

While it can be said that treated surfaces and stylish fixtures are the bones of a beautiful bathroom, it is what one might call the "extras" that fill out the space, giving it a look and personality all its own. They soften the room's edges and warm its practical nature. They bring light and life to what would otherwise be a predictably staged shell equipped with the room's necessities. Thanks to the extras—furniture, accessories, stylized lighting—there is no such thing as a typical bathroom. The space has been dressed up, opening its doors to decorative elements once thought off-limits to the space. These pieces help turn the simple bathroom into a showcase in which to relax, read, and retreat. Among them are comfortable armchairs, brilliant sconces, and sink-topped chests. Swank accessories include sparkling decanters, exquisite paintings, and sensational objects once displayed only in the home's living areas. Anything goes as today's bath welcomes ingenuity and individualized design. And while the bathroom will always house its essential pipes and plumbing, it's the extras that put an exclamation point on the room's personal statement of style.

Mention the words bathroom furniture and you may be met with a blank stare. A hamper, vanity, or stool, yes, . . . but furniture? As the bathroom has evolved from a characterless closet into a personal retreat, furniture enjoyed in other rooms of the home has become a natural here. A comfortable armchair, a chest of drawers, and a sumptuous chaise reflect your personal style as they invite you to unwind in beauty and comfort. Smaller pieces can also be used to enhance the experience of the bath. A valet stand or coatrack adds character while offering a place to hang the day's jacket, a fluffy robe, or thirsty towels. A bookshelf or accent table by the tub provides a convenient and attractive place to hold your favorite book, candles, and telephone. An upholstered bench

FURNITURE

placed in front of a vanity mirror is the perfect place to perch and prepare for the day. Consider how you plan to spend time in your bath and use furnishings, large and small, to enrich and personalize the home's newly defined bath/living room.

Freestanding furniture pieces are both practical and decorative additions to the bathroom. They open the room to limitless design possibilities while providing additional storage, comfortable seating, and mobile surfaces for placement and display. As in other rooms, a bathroom's furnishings are major contributors to creating the desired décor and ambience of the space. A chrome-framed chaise shouts "modern" just as a period dressing table whispers of an era gone by. Even small pedestals, benches, and accent tables can make enormous stylistic statements in the bathroom. Furniture can also be used to upstage or conceal the room's basic functions and redefine the purpose of the space. Is it a lounge or sitting room? Maybe it is an exercise area or meditative space. By introducing distinctive furniture to the bathroom—pieces that characterize a non-bath space—the antiquated expectations of the standard bathroom go up in smoke. The bath becomes whatever you decide. Furniture can also be used to hide or house an essential fixture. Antique chests and beautiful armoires become the hosts for sinks and plumbing. Set into a marble-topped bureau or behind the doors of a beautiful armoire, the basin takes on a whole new dimension. Even the simplest of chairs can become a cherished addition to a bathroom. It can perform as a shelf for a stack of fluffy towels, a place to drape a piece of clothing, or simply a spot to sit while bathing the dog.

PAGE 101
Handsome twin chests smartly serve as a vanity and stone-topped bureau in the inverted corner of this charming bath.

OPPOSITE
Comfort comes in many forms in today's bath. This eclectic retreat enlists a luxuriously upholstered chaise to provide a place to lounge, while it softens the "edgy" character of the room's other features.

LEFT
Scale plus style add up to make this enormous sideboard the perfect piece of furniture upon which to place the one-of-a-kind double sink. To balance the visual weight of the "fixture," two heavily framed mirrors are hung above.

Ample and well-placed storage is the key to a successful bathroom. It provides a hideaway for unsightly amenities from lotions to tissues, leaving the space open to display your favorite objects and accessories. Conventional fitted cabinetry and vanities offer drawers and concealed storage below the countertop surface. They are convenient and easily accessible. For baths with wall-mounted, pedestal, or open-console sinks, a stroke of creativity may be necessary to supply storage to the active bath. A charming chest or dresser can be used for drawer space for toiletries and cosmetics. Open shelves—built-in, mounted, freestanding—are a great place to display the more appealing of the bath's necessities. Colorful towels, herbal soaps, linens, and loofahs are perfect here. Many of the room's less attractive items—cotton balls and swabs, razors, creams and gels—can become objets d'art when stored and displayed in sparkling glass canisters and apothecary jars. Mobile carts, hampers, baskets, decorative boxes, and small trunks offer portable storage space as well as an opportunity to influence the room with their character. Of course, the traditional medicine cabinet—not so traditional in today's updated and spectacular versions—mirrors the beauty of the space while stowing a plenitude of the bath's unattractive essentials. Finally, well-placed hooks, rods, and railings furnish places to hang anything from towels to robes, wood-handled brushes to the proverbial soap-on-a-rope.

UPPER LEFT
Stylishly spare, this bathroom uses colorful, wall-mounted cabinets, and even below-the-mirror cubbyhole drawers to provide ample storage for the space. By keeping them all elevated above the floor, the room retains its open, spacious feel.

LOWER LEFT
What appears to be a bank of drawers, when under the counter, in this gleaming fitted cabinetry turns out to be a softly cushioned bench that serves the vanity with inventive style.

OPPOSITE
A handsome leather-covered chest of drawers furnishes substantial storage and enormous style to this character-rich bathroom.

THE FIRST EMPEROR OF CHINA

The world is but a canvas to the imagination.

Anonymous

Say good-bye to the characterless cabinetry and boring vanities of the past. Today, handsome chests and beautiful bureaus are becoming the rage for the high-style bath. Functionally, they provide an abundance of storage space while decoratively, they set the tone and personality of the room. If it can be fitted with plumbing and accommodate a sink, it is fair game. Consider a salvaged chest of drawers with crackled paint for a seaside- or country-style bath. Just as perfect, an antique cabinet adds authenticity to an old-world-style powder room. A heavily carved sideboard can be fitted with double sinks to become the focal point of a grand master bath. Each stands ready to be converted into an engaging fixture that oozes with style and personality.

LEFT
By converting a classically styled bow-front chest into a single-sink vanity, this simple powder room is transformed into a stunning and sophisticated space.

OPPOSITE
Lavishly detailed, this powder room boasts an unforgettable vanity fashioned from a handsomely detailed chest of drawers. It is perfectly fitted with a small bowl and period hardware.

In the bathroom, accessories are objects that range from purely decorative to entirely practical. From a simple bar of soap to a one-of-a-kind crystal vase, each has the potential to enliven the look and feel of the room. They bring color, texture, and character to the space. Because the bath is first and foremost

ACCESSORIES

a functionally defined room, it has many items that are necessities. When these items are thoughtfully chosen and displayed, they can wash the bathroom with personality. A stack of fluffy towels, a bowl of bath beads, a basket of loofahs, sea sponges, and wood-handled brushes, all lend style to the room. Of course, ornamental objects have the same power. Brilliantly colored artwork, vintage ceramics, sparkling glassware, and one-of-a-kind architectural remnants are just a few of the endless possibilities. Remember, accessories once thought off-limits in the bath are now welcomed with open arms. Anything that brings you joy and adds a bit of pizzazz is the perfect addition to the finely detailed bathroom.

Decorative accessories celebrate your unique style while imparting immense personality to the bath. When determining whether a particular accessory fits in your bathroom, consider whether the object is pleasing to you. Does it make you smile? Also, how does it affect the room? Does it stylistically complement the look or theme of the space? This is important. Just as an ideal accessory can accentuate the intended nature of your bath, an ill-fitting object can actually interrupt its distinct style. For example, if you are designing a serene Zen-like bath, a simple raku pot is very fitting, while a faceted crystal vase or boldly colored painting is not. Every object possesses unique inherent qualities—color, texture, finish, form, size. Consider these qualities as you place an item in the room. Fortunately, accessorizing is a trial-and-error practice that allows you to try again. If a piece doesn't fit, place it elsewhere and take a chance with another alternative item. With a keen and imaginative eye, you can find and place the perfect accessories to make your own unique statement of style.

LEFT
The carefully selected accessories in this peaceful bath accentuate the room's texture-rich nature without adding excess clutter. By creatively placing the carved wooden angel on a small stand, the figure becomes more prominent and, size-wise, is more fitting for the space.

OPPOSITE
A brilliant painting and a selection of distinctive pots are used to add decorative punch to this bathroom. Their complementary colors, the dried floral arrangements, and the exotic motifs of the mirror frame combine to make this room an exhilarating sight.

In few other rooms do practical objects add so much to the décor. Thoughtfully chosen everyday "must haves" of the bath—soap dishes, bottled oils, towels and the like—can contribute enormous character to the room. Because the limited space of the bathroom often restricts the number of decorative accessories it can accommodate, it sometimes becomes the task of the essential amenities to add flavor.

Overlook nothing when considering the impact these items can bring to your bath. What works best, . . . a nickel- or brass-plated towel ring? A towel neatly folded on a glass rod or casually draped from a porcelain hook? A bath mat of dark wooden slats or thick, plush carpeting? A wicker or chrome-framed laundry basket? And what about the hair and body soaps, lotions, creams, and oils? A clear glycerin bar or opaque block of milled soap, each makes a different stylistic statement. So does a bowl of glistening white salts or richly colored bath beads. Choose wisely. And what about their display? An eyesore when left in half-empty plastic containers and label-ridden jars, these elements shine when shown off in glass bottles and iridescent decanters.

OPPOSITE
When dressed up, eye-catching accessories—silver-handled brushes, distinctive soap and cup holders, wooden bowls, textured towels, fluted drinking glasses—can help transform a simple bath setting into a pronouncement of distinctive style.

RIGHT
The pure and understated beauty of this bathroom is articulated by minimal clutter and the honest display of detail. Even hanging towels become an effective part of its simple presentation.

Five hundred years ago, the Venetians perfected the process of creating pure glass that is flawlessly clear and colorless. Since then, rooms throughout the ages have been brilliantly accessorized with the radiant beauty of this material. Today's bath is no exception. Sparkling bottles, translucent containers, and airy decanters of all shapes and sizes create dramatic and eye-catching displays. What's more, when filled with colorful gels, salts, and lotions, glass vessels come alive with the color and texture of their contents. Numerous glass pieces are best displayed in collections or groups. They lose their impact when spread independently throughout the room. Placing them under direct light, on a reflective tray, or in front of a mirror also intensifies their lustrous beauty.

LEFT
A diverse grouping of sizes, shapes, and styles makes this collection of translucent and luminous decanters a stunning and sparkling display.

RIGHT
Glass, in all its brilliance, is used throughout this bathroom to create delightfully dazzling décor. The beauty of the sparkling accessories—decanters, vases, bottles, and even beaded lamp shades—reflect on glass shower walls and the mirrored surfaces of the glittering dressing table.

In the bath, decorative mirrors and radiant lighting pair like perfect partners to illuminate the space with character and personality. They work in tandem to brighten the room, to enlarge it visually, and to reflect its distinctive style. And, while versions of each can be found throughout the room, it is over the vanity that

MIRRORS & LIGHTS

they come together to perform their real magic. Here they create the bath's most recognized focal point. They stylishly frame and light this most-frequented area of the room. Functionally, one can't overemphasize the importance of good lighting for a mirrored vanity. It is, after all, where we groom and primp before stepping out into the world. The vanity is where lighting and mirrors merge to flavor the bathroom. Their size, shape, and style are all important to the impact they make on the space. So is the way they relate to one another. Ornately shaded fixtures paired with a gilded rococo-framed looking glass cause an elaborately elegant bath to shine. On the other hand, a free-form, unframed mirror accented with suspended halogen lights creates a much more contemporary and artsy pronouncement. The options and combinations are infinite. Whatever your style, utilize the mirrors and lighting of your vanity to create a look that reflects well upon you and your distinctive bathroom.

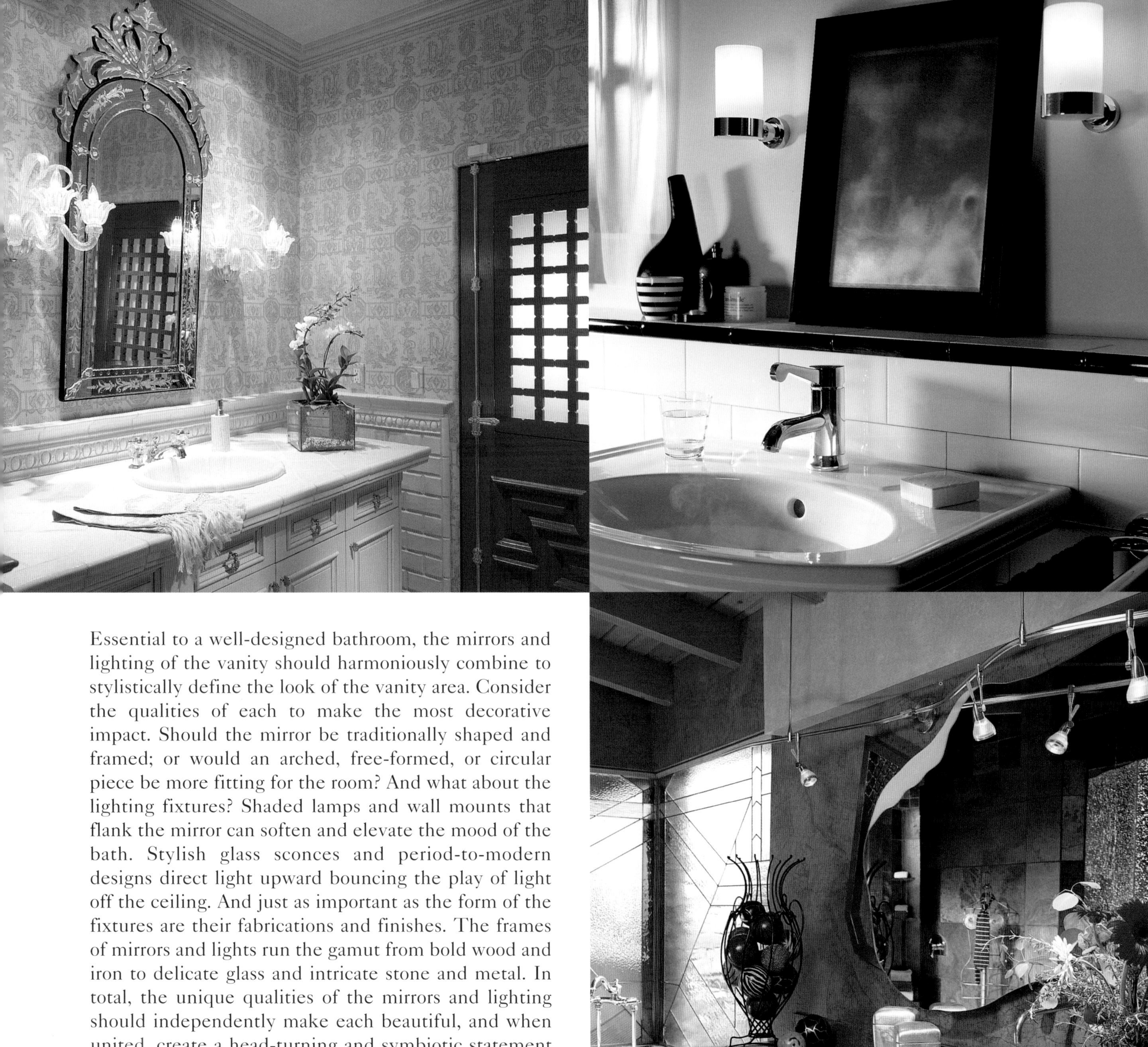

Essential to a well-designed bathroom, the mirrors and lighting of the vanity should harmoniously combine to stylistically define the look of the vanity area. Consider the qualities of each to make the most decorative impact. Should the mirror be traditionally shaped and framed; or would an arched, free-formed, or circular piece be more fitting for the room? And what about the lighting fixtures? Shaded lamps and wall mounts that flank the mirror can soften and elevate the mood of the bath. Stylish glass sconces and period-to-modern designs direct light upward bouncing the play of light off the ceiling. And just as important as the form of the fixtures are their fabrications and finishes. The frames of mirrors and lights run the gamut from bold wood and iron to delicate glass and intricate stone and metal. In total, the unique qualities of the mirrors and lighting should independently make each beautiful, and when united, create a head-turning and symbiotic statement of undeniable style.

PAGE 117
A series of lovely mirrors is used to both accentuate this room's unique shape and to reflect the beauty of the ornately scrolled, shaded sconces.

OPPOSITE UPPER LEFT
A symmetrically scrolled crest and reverse-etched borders beautifully detail this classic Venetian mirror. Ornate Italian glass sconces are paired with the mirror to finely finish the elegant look.

OPPOSITE UPPER RIGHT
An unmounted black-framed mirror, when paired with modern cylindrical sconces, makes a simple, yet commanding focal point above this contemporary sink.

OPPOSITE LOWER RIGHT
Created like a piece of modern art, this bathroom mirror is uniquely shaped and backed by an abstract wall sculpture. Adjustable halogen lighting performs on a high wire to accentuate the mirror and the free-wheeling design of the entire room.

LEFT
This mirror's hand-forged frame and pair of shaded, iron wall lamps turn an ordinary wall into a visual statement of style. United, they perfectly balance the dramatically lighted figure recessed in a neighboring niche.

PURPOSE

What is the role you intend for your bathroom? Is it your personal private sanctuary, or will it be open to family and guests? Is it a full-scale spa or an intimate powder room? Does it double as a changing space, exercise room, sitting area, or laundry? The answer to these questions can help determine the details that, when combined, create a tailor-made bath that looks and performs especially for you. Differently defined bathrooms present unique and divergent opportunities for detail. Powder rooms invite dramatic and theatrical design, while guest and family baths embrace warmth and comfort. Further, the master bath is truly personal and deserves to be dressed with anything and everything that helps make it your exclusive retreat. The key is to determine how and by whom the room will be used and indulge in the infinite details that create a bath that is uniquely yours.

Diminutive, compact, snug. . . the powder room may be small in size, but it is huge in decorative potential. By its very nature, it invites the most dramatic details. First, the restricted size of the room accommodates daring, flavorful treatments that would be unthinkable in larger doses. Brilliant colors, bold textures, and fearless accents are among the unforgettable elements that bring this room to life. Second, because the powder room is normally used for short periods of time, over-the-top details that might be unpleasant with prolonged exposure, work their magical charm during shorter visits to the room. Finally, unlike the master or guest baths that are normally

POWDER ROOM

decoratively tied to adjoining rooms, the powder room need not coordinate or complement adjacent spaces in the home. It can don a persona all its own. It is like a lone jewel waiting to dazzle all who enter.

Big things come in small packages.

Anonymous

In the powder room, be courageous with detail. This is the bath in which you set your imagination free. Here, function follows form. Because of the room's limited use and purpose, the decorative qualities of its fixtures and features should be free to overshadow their practicality. Look to every fixture, surface, accent, and accessory as an opportunity to unleash your uninhibited sense of style on this smallest of baths. The dramatic results promise to be enormous!

PAGE 123
In this extraordinary cave-like bathroom, raw, primitive detail touches each and every feature. For a space so purely primeval, the civilized term "powder room" seems hardly fitting.

FAR LEFT
This dazzling powder room uses an imaginatively designed glass-based vanity, clear glass sink, and large decorative mirror to create a spacious feel, while giving the room a one-of-a-kind look.

CENTER LEFT
A single feature can turn a powder room from ordinary to extraordinary. A stone bowl cradled by a spreading branch creates drama while tying the room decoratively to the exterior hallway.

LEFT
The permanence and power of stone give this richly carved vanity everlasting beauty. To keep the large feature from being overwhelming in this tight space, the area beneath the sink is left empty and the generously sized mirror is built-in and accented with shaded sconces.

LEFT
Leather-bound books, a framed timepiece, and warmly finished wainscoting add a masculine feel to the sink area.

LOWER RIGHT
Decorated like a classic gentleman's club, this bathroom enlists the help of a period console, timeless fittings, wood, and even plaid to produce the polished, genteel look.

LOWER LEFT
Characteristic of the 1920s, this classy bathroom features a highly stylized console and stunning ceramic and glass tile that fashion its sophisticated appeal.

OPPOSITE
The clean silhouette of custom cabinetry, tailored hardware, black marble countertop, and smartly positioned lighting give this highly stylized, yet understated bathroom a masculine flair.

A hand towel that reads "HIS" across the bottom does not prefer the company of bubble bath and crystal perfume bottles. It is better suited for a room with a penchant for more masculine detail.

HIS

Enter: the man's bathroom. This is a room created for the male of the species. Its fixtures, finishes, accents, and accessories are warm but not soft, inviting but not indulgent. Where a woman's bath pampers and coddles, a man's bath relaxes and rejuvenates. If a choice between a shower or tub must be made, the shower wins every time. Richly stained and polished woods enrich the space. Deep shades and natural colors are favored. Pattern, when it is used, leans toward plaids, stripes, or geometrics. Chrome or brass hardware complement veined marbles and natural stone. Lighting is task-oriented; and while stylistic fixtures are incorporated, they are not chosen for providing a soft, muted glow. Accessories are practical in nature. From unpatterned towels and a ceramic shaving mug to a clear glass tumbler and tortoiseshell comb, each has a functional purpose. Family photos and books personalize the room. A favorite chair, small TV, and sound system add to the room's enjoyment level. Detail is kept simple and straightforward, timeless and uncluttered. Such is the nature of "HIS" bathroom.

For each woman there is her own idea of the perfect bath; a truly personal retreat created solely for her. For some, the idyllic bath is a private sanctuary that

HERS

soothes and softens at the day's end. It is a blissful, intimate space that indulges all the senses. Visually, the room is rich in calming yet lavish detail. Color runs the gamut from quiet, blushing tones to vivid hues of blossoming springtime gardens. Honey-toned marble or stone flooring, softly sponged walls, and molded ceilings grace the room. Draped shower curtains and window dressings are partnered with sheers and vintage laces. A claw-footed tub is surrounded by an eclectic mix of furnishings and accent pieces—a painted side chair stacked with tea towels, a charming flea-market chest, a slip-covered vanity chair, and an irresistible chaise that entices after-bath lounging. Shaded lamps and elegant sconces create a mellowed, romantic atmosphere. Antique gild-framed mirrors, vintage prints, botanicals, and a touch of trompe l'oeil accent the walls. Collections of sparkling crystal perfume bottles, bowls of scented soaps, clusters of candles, and a grouping of antique brushes are favored accessories. A vase of roses finishes the room perfectly.

RIGHT
An abundance of posh feminine accents fill this large bathroom with a woman's touch. Plants, shaded wall lamps, and slip-covered chairs soften the hard edges of the stone walls and unadorned windows.

OPPOSITE UPPER RIGHT
Just a few perfectly chosen accessories can bring a sense of romance and beauty to any bathroom.

OPPOSITE LOWER RIGHT
A weave of tea roses embellishes the graceful sink and antique faucet of this lovely vanity. Delicate accessories finish the feminine look.

JaneAvril
de Paris

"The Great Escape". . . a fitting title for today's master bath. For the "owners" of the home, it provides a much-anticipated, nonpublic space to unwind and refresh. It is their retreat and, as such, is one of the most cherished spaces under roof. Because of its inherently private nature, it invites design and detail that is uniquely personal. This makes it impossible to describe the single most perfect master bath. It all depends on whose room it is. Common to all well-designed master baths are fixtures, fittings, surfaces, and accents selected purely for the pleasure of the masters of the home. Consideration of guests or other family members is irrelevant.

MASTER BATH

Regardless of its size, large or small, the ideal master bath thrives on unique and treasured details. Often the look and feel of the room originates in the master bedroom and flows into the bath. The result is a fluidly decorated master suite. It boasts complementary and coordinating surface treatments, colors, accents, and accessories that unite the two areas. On the other hand, the master bath can be decorated independently of the bedroom and feature elements and amenities that make it a one-of-a-kind getaway that pampers and relaxes. In either case, the room should be designed and detailed solely for those who use it. After all, it is their private paradise.

Luxury must be comfortable, otherwise it is not a luxury.

Coco Chanel

PAGE 131
Epitomizing the hallmark of today's master bath, this room is spacious, richly accented, and luxuriously furnished. It takes its decorative lead from the master bedroom and incorporates many of its details. The floor plan and countertop layout are designed to comfortably accommodate two people at once.

RIGHT
What is more indulgent than a bathside fireplace? Add to this a plush armchair and a scenic view, and you have created a bath that is destined to become the favorite room in the home.

OPPOSITE
Large-scale details are very important in sizable, well-designed master baths. This immense space boasts an impressive ceiling treatment that visually lowers the surface while adding immeasurable character to the room. A substantial built-in tub and solid cabinetry add needed weight to the space, while heavy carvings and bold patterns on the rug and bench introduce comforting texture and color.

Comfort is the hallmark of the evolved master bath. This alone can turn it from a hit-and-run pit stop to a haven one hesitates to leave.

BOTTOM LEFT
A quiet tub and a basket of thick, thirsty towels defines private time in this understated bath.

RIGHT
Simple and serene, . . . an all-white bathroom furnished with a favorite chair is a sublime solution to relieve stress.

OPPOSITE
With all the charm and ease of a sun-filled porch, this master bath relies on banks of undressed windows, plank floors, timeworn furnishings, and cherished collectibles to create its undeniable allure. A shade of white washes the room with an honest simplicity, and acts as the perfect backdrop for the beauty of the outdoor view.

The simplification of anything is always sensational.

Anonymous

It's no secret, the home plays an important part in the quality of life that we lead. It more than provides shelter, it surrounds us with a sense of who we are. When you dress a room with the materials, colors, and objects that you love, it becomes a reflection of your unique style and taste. The bathroom is no exception. It has as much decorative potential as any other room in the house. In fact, because it is such a private space, the bath invites even more personal and indulgent treatments than the home's more public spaces.

Now that you have seen the many ways that an everyday bathroom can be transformed into a space bursting with life and character, it is time to turn your sights toward your own bath. Envision it as you never have before. Look beyond its practical nature. Douse it with a generous dose of imaginative detail. The result will be a one-of-a-kind retreat that is alive with your own personal sense of style.

Brad Mee is a writer and author, who specializes in interiors and homes. His background in design includes both interior and fashion design, as well as home furnishings and advertising. *Bathrooms: Design Is in the Details* is the third of a publication series he has created. It follows *Kitchens: Design Is in the Details* and *Design Is in the Details*. Brad is the editor of *Utah Style & Design Magazine* and divides his time between Salt Lake City, Utah, and Phoenix, Arizona.

From the Author

I would like to express my appreciation to everyone who made this book possible. My thanks go to the imaginative designers, architects, builders, manufacturers, and artisans whose work is showcased throughout these pages. This book is a credit to their talent and creativity. Special thanks also to the extraordinary photographers who captured the magic of their work and to the gracious home owners who opened their doors to share the beauty of their bathrooms. I am especially grateful to my friends and colleagues at Chapelle, Ltd., for their continuing and enthusiastic support and to my skilled editor, Karmen Quinney, who is a delight to work with and, once again, proved herself indispensable. Thank-you, as well, to David Miller and Lydia Cutter for their generous input. I would also like to recognize *Phoenix Home & Garden Magazine* for the numerous images shown that were originally featured in that publication. The talents of editor Linda J. Barkman and art director Margie Van Zee are much appreciated. Finally, I am especially indebted to photographer Dino Tonn for his remarkable talent and the whole-hearted dedication he has brought to the book.

ACKNOWLEDGMENTS

The author would like to thank the following for contributing photography to this book:

Dino Tonn Photography
5433 East Kathleen Road
Phoenix, Arizona 85254
(602) 765-0455
An attention to detail and true artistry in lighting have made Dino Tonn one of the leading architectural photographers in the Southwest. Specializing in award-winning architectural and golf-course photography, Tonn has been photographing much of the Southwest's finest architecture for the past 13 years. He serves clients in the hospitality field as well as architects, interior designers, developers, and many other design-related businesses and publications. His work has been featured in regional and national publications. Tonn is a native of Arizona and resides in Scottsdale, Arizona, with his wife and two children.

Lydia Cutter – Photographer
1029 North George Mason Drive
Arlington, Virginia 22205
(703) 741-0424
A specialist in interior photography, Lydia Cutter has been serving residential and commercial clients nationally for over 21 years. In addition to her photography, she also produces fine art that adorns both beautiful homes and unique commercial buildings throughout the country. Her photographic work has been featured in national and regional interior publications. Cutter now resides in Arlington, Virginia.

Scot Zimmerman – Photographer
P.O. Box 289
261 North 400 West
Heber City, Utah 84032–0289
(800) 654-7897/zimfolks@sprynet.com
Scot Zimmerman is an architectural photographer. During the last 20 years, his accomplishments include: photographing and producing six books, having his photographs featured in over 46 books, regular contributions to national and regional architectural and home & garden publications, and ongoing assignments across the country. Six museums have exhibited his work.

Bill Timmerman – Photographer
382 North 1st Avenue
Phoenix, Arizona 85003
(602) 420-9325
A professional photographer for 25 years, Bill Timmerman's primary focus became architectural photography after his images of the Phoenix Central Library (architect Will Bruder) were published internationally. His ever expanding clientele includes accomplished contemporary architects and interior designers. He has been a resident of Phoenix, Arizona, for 16 years.

David Michael Miller Associates
7034 East First Avenue
Scottsdale, Arizona 85251
(480) 425-7545
A custom interior design studio committed to creating unique and beautiful environments for its clients.

Paul Schatz
Interior Design Imports
San Diego, California
(619) 696-6373
Paul Schatz, principal of Interior Design Imports leads a design team recognized for consistently delivering the highest level of design expertise in an organized and professional manner. The IDI design team explores a wide range of styles with an emphasis on interior architectural detailing, bridging the gap between architect, builder, and designer.

Ann Sacks
(800)278-8453/www.annsacks.com
From the well-worn beauty of centuries-old marble to the whimsical spirit of one-of-a-kind art tiles, inspirational designs have made Ann Sacks number one in fine tile and stone products. That leadership now extends to luxury plumbing products that are both thrilling and unexpected.

Dornbracht
(800) 774-1181/www.dornbracht.com
Dornbracht combines design with substance: beneath each exclusive finish such as chrome, platinum, or gold, designed to give each item the appearance of a customer's choice, there is solid brass. Such high-grade materials and sound craftsmanship are the very substance and expression of the Dornbracht product's durability and function.

Duravit AG
78128 Hornberg, Germany
+49/7833/70-0/www.duravit.com
In its efforts to supply a genuinely comprehensive range, Duravit accords priority to ensuring variety in products for the bathroom, which is virtually unparalleled on the sanitaryware market. From basic forms to designer bathrooms from Philippe Starck, Michael Graves, Massimo Iosa Ghini, Sieger Design, and Norman Foster, Duravit covers all possible budgets and lifestyles.

Kohler Co.
(800)-4-KOHLER
www.KOHLER.com
Since 1873, Kohler has been a pioneer of new styles, innovative technologies, and colors that stand the test of time. Kohler continues to provide well-designed, reliable kitchen and bath products that enhance one's lifestyle, are attainable and easy to live with, and perform with a high level of quality.

CREDITS

KEY
(l) = left
(r) = right
(u) = upper
(l) = lower
(ctr) = center

PHOTOGRAPHY

Lydia Cutter 22–23, 24, 40–41, 45, 49, 56–57, 63, 69

Bill Timmerman 13, 26–27, 29(lr), 38(r), 62, 77(ur), 78, 80(lr), 113, 144

Dino Tonn 2, 3(ll), 4–5, 6(l), 7(ctr) (r), 11, 15, 21, 28–29, 35, 39, 43, 44, 46–48, 50(ll) (ur), 51–52, 53(ll) (lr) (ur), 54–55, 58, 59(ll) (ur), 60–61, 64(ul), 65, 71, 74(ur), 75, 79, 81, 82(ul) (lr), 83–85, 89–90, 91(ll) (ur), 92(ul), 94(lr), 95, 96(ur) (ll), 99, 101, 102–103, 104(ll), 105–111, 115, 117, 118(ul) (lr), 119–120, 123, 124(l) (r), 125, 127–133

Margie Van Zee (photostylist) 2, 35, 60, 71, 75, 81, 84–85, 89, 94(ul), 99, 101, 106–107, 110, 115, 118(lr), 120, 123, 124(r), 125, 128–129, 132

Scot Zimmerman 42

INTERIOR DESIGN

Bess Jones Interiors, Scottsdale, AZ 91(ur), 96(ur), 124(l), 125

Billi Springer Interior Design, Scottsdale, AZ 99, 110, 132

Bron Design Group, Phoenix, AZ
Dorothy & Eric Bron 7(r), 59(ll), 89, 120

Carol Minchew Interiors, Scottsdale, AZ
Carol Minchew 2, 48, 64(ul), 107

Casa del Encanto, Scottsdale, AZ
Luis Corona & Michael Barron 40–41, 45, 71, 82(lr)

Chipley Construction, Scottsdale, AZ
Melinda Chipley 79

Christopher Coffin, 7(ctr), 101

Conquest, Sherry 84

David Michael Miller Associates, Scottsdale, AZ
David Michael Miller 3(ll), 13, 26–27, 29(lr), 38(r), 54, 62, 77(ur), 78, 80(lr), 113, 119, 144

Dawson Design Associates, Phoenix, AZ
Maria Dawson 108–109

Debra May Himes Interior Design & Associates, Mesa, AZ 94(lr)

Do Daz Inc. Design Firm, Scottsdale, AZ
Teri Mulmed 44, 61

European Design, Scottsdale, AZ
Allan Rosenthal 50(ll)

Ferraras Interiors, Scottsdale, AZ
Gaye Ferrara 43, 102(l)

Friedman & Shields, Scottsdale, AZ 65, 130–131

Interior Design Imports
Paul Schatz 64(lr), 74(lr)

Jamie Herzlinger Interiors, Scottsdale, AZ 28–29, 58, 59(ur), 118(ul), 127

Jones Studio Inc., Phoenix, AZ
Eddie Jones 35

Kuemmel, Lisa, Salt Lake City, UT 42

Magee, Peter, Scottsdale, AZ 4–5, 15, 50(ur)

Mee, Brad 73(ur) (lr), 122

Miller Old World Building Design, Scottsdale, AZ
Clint Miller 74

Nancy Hepburn Interiors, Paradise Valley, AZ 52–53, 96(ll)

North Peak Design, Scottsdale, AZ
Donna Haugen 83, 95

Paula Berg Design Associates, Scottsdale, AZ
Paula Berg 22–24, 49, 63, 69

Paula Designs, Scottsdale, AZ
Paula den Boer 11

Robb & Stucky Design Studio, Scottsdale, AZ
Judy Marshall 105

Sally J. Schaefer Interior Design, Scottsdale, AZ 111

Smith & Dana Associates, Scottsdale, AZ
Carol Smith 55, 85, 92(ul)

Spaceline Design 82(ul)

Treken Interiors, Paradise Valley, AZ
Kimberly Fisher-Colletti 21

Trent Gasbarra Design, Scottsdale, AZ
Trent Gasbarra 104(ll)

Vallone Design Inc., Scottsdale, AZ
Donna Vallone 106, 115

Wendy Black Rogers, Paradise Valley, AZ 56–57

Wiseman & Gale Interiors, Scottsdale, AZ
Sue Calvin 123
Jane Parker Lee 133

ARCHITECTS

Allen Tafoya AIA, Carefree, AZ 110, 132

Architekton, Tempe, AZ 102(l)

Brissette Architects Inc., Scottsdale, AZ 48, 107
Chipley Construction, Scottsdale, AZ 79
H&S International, Scottsdale, AZ 117
Harris Design Co., Scottsdale, AZ
Ward Harris 118(lr)
Mittelstaedt, Grover & Cooper Ltd., Phoenix, AZ
Jan Mittelstaedt 75
Jeff Page Architect, Scottsdale, AZ 82(ul)
Jones Studio, Inc., Phoenix, AZ
Eddie Jones 35
Lash McDaniel 123
Miller Associates Old World Building Design, Scottsdale, AZ
Clint Miller 74
R.J. Bacon Company, Phoenix, AZ
Bob Bacon Architectural Designer 7(r), 59(ll), 89, 120
Rick Daugherty Architect, Scottsdale, AZ 6(l), 39, 81, 90
Tamara Pohle Architect, Scottsdale, AZ 119
Urban Design Associates, Scottsdale, AZ 52–53, 91(ur), 96(ll), 124(l)
Wes Balmer, Phoenix, AZ 133

BUILDERS

Arnette Romero, Inc. Builders, Scottsdale, AZ 132
Cal Christiansen Custom Homes, Scottsdale, AZ 133
Chipley Construction, Scottsdale, AZ 79
DeLellis Development Group, Carefree, AZ 119
Denniston & Company, Scottsdale, AZ 102(l)
Forte Homes, Scottsdale, AZ 94(lr)
Gietz Master Builders, Scottsdale, AZ 71
Hayes Martin Design & Development, Scottsdale, AZ 55, 85, 92(ul)
Kitchell Custom Homes, Phoenix, AZ 7(r), 59(ll), 89
Legacy Custom Builders, Scottsdale, AZ 84, 102–103
Magee Custom Homes, LLC., Scottsdale, AZ 4–5, 15, 50(ur)
Minchew Corp., Scottsdale, AZ 64(ul)
Nance Construction, Phoenix, AZ 117
North Peak Construction, Scottsdale, AZ 83, 95
P. Stark Builders, Scottsdale, AZ
Paul Stark 120
Phil Smith Construction, Carefree, AZ 48, 107
Phoenix Smith, Scottsdale, AZ 130–131
RS Homes, Scottsdale, AZ 51
Salcito Custom Homes, LTD., Scottsdale, AZ 61, 96(ur), 125
Shiloh Custom Homes, Scottsdale, AZ 11

CABINET DESIGN

Architectural Wood Interiors 133
Beams Designs, Phoenix, AZ
Don Beams 102(l)
Casa del Encanto, Scottsdale, AZ 82(lr)
European Design, Scottsdale, AZ
Allan Rosenthal 50(ll), 104(ll)
Keisler Enterprises, Phoenix, AZ 91(ur)

OTHER TRADES

Dennis Hopper Walls, Phoenix, AZ 123
Legendary Fine Finishes, Scottsdale, AZ - Wall Finishes 2, 11
Stockett Tile & Granite 3(ll), 4–5, 15, 50(ur), 54
Touch of Glass - Glasswork 64(ul)

PRODUCTS

Ann Sacks 3(ul), 72, 136–137
Dornbracht 6(ctr), 12, 32, 34(ul), 36, 37(ll) (lr) (ur), 38(ctr l) (ll), 59(lr), 70(ul), 76, 77(ll), 80(ul), 93(lr), 112(lr), 116, 118(ur), 139
Duravit 1, 8, 34(lr), 38(ul), 91(ul), 93(ll), 104(ul), 112(ll), 135
Kohler *Photography courtesy of Kohler Co.* 6, 7(ctr), 14(ul) (ll), 16, 18(ul) (ll), 19, 25(ll) (ur), 30(lr), 31, 33, 67, 70(ll), 77(lr), 86, 87(ll) (lr) (ur), 92(lr), 93(ul), 94(ul) (ll), 96(ul) (lr), 97, 100, 126(ul) (ll) (lr), 129(lr)

PHOTODISKS

Corbis Corporation Images (© 1999) 23(lr)
Photodisc, Inc. Images (© 1999) 17(ur) (lr) (ll), 18(ur), 20, 25(lr), 28(ll), 29(ur), 30(ul), 73(ll), 77(ul), 112(ul) (ur), 114, 129(ur), 134(ll) (r), 142–143

Every effort has been made to credit all contributors. We apologize in advance for any unintentional omission and would be pleased to insert the appropriate acknowledgment in any subsequent edition.

INDEX

Accessories 108–115

Acknowledgments. 138–139

Auden, W.H 18

Bath 68–75

Bowl(s). 14, 34, 88–90, 92, 94–95, 107–108, 113

Ceilings 62–65

Chanel, Coco. 132

Classic Style 26–32

Claw-footed tub(s). 22, 66, 128

Console(s) 28, 33, 88, 90, 92 94, 104

Credits 140–141

da Vinci, Leonardo 37

Decanter(s). 20, 34, 98, 113–114

Emerson, Ralph Waldo. 97

Extras. 98–119

Fantasy Style. 40–45

Faux finishes. 22, 50

Fixtures 66–97

Flagstone 54, 59, 74, 81, 84

Floors. 56–61

Focal point(s) 33, 45, 58, 90, 94, 107, 116, 119

Furniture 9, 20, 100–107

Glass 9, 14, 18, 28, 33–34, 48, 50, 60, 73–74, 78, 80, 82, 84, 86, 88, 92, 114, 116, 118, 125, 127

Hardware. 18, 22, 30, 34, 51, 66, 70, 74, 76–78, 87, 90, 94, 97, 107, 127

Hers 128–129

His 126–127

Jeffries, Richard 16

Introduction 8–9

Lavatory. 14, 50, 90, 92, 94

Luxury Style 20–25

Master Bath 130–135

Mirror(s) 16, 18, 22, 25, 34, 42, 45, 50–52, 64, 90, 104, 110, 116, 118–119, 125, 128

Mirrors & Lights 116–119

Modern Style. 33–39

Monochromatic 14, 28, 80

Nature. 16–17, 23, 30, 74, 98, 127

Outdoor shower(s). 84

Palette 28

Pattern(s). 14, 26, 37, 56, 58–60, 64, 80, 127

Pedestal 30, 33, 66, 88, 90–91, 104

Plant(s) 20, 22–23, 45, 51, 128

Powder Room. . . 9, 20, 64, 107, 121–125

Purpose 120–135

Shell 46–65

Shower. 9, 18, 22, 34, 37, 66, 78–87, 114, 127–128

Shower door(s) 16, 86

Showerheads 14, 18, 82, 87

Sinks. 88–97

Skylights 30, 62, 64

Small bath 14, 16, 56, 91–93

Smith, Logan Pearsall. 25

Stone 9, 12, 14, 16–17, 30, 33–34, 40, 42, 45–46, 48, 50, 54, 56, 58, 60, 73–74, 78, 80–81, 86, 90, 118, 125, 128

Storage 90–93, 103–104, 107

Style. 10–45

Spa Style 12–19

Texture(s) . . 9, 16–17, 20, 30, 34, 51, 54, 56, 59–60, 64, 74, 108, 110, 113–114, 132

Towel rack(s) 23, 26, 34, 38

Trompe l'oeil 53, 62, 128

Vanity(s) 22, 33, 42, 51, 54, 60, 90, 92, 100, 104, 107, 116, 125, 128

Venetian mirror 119

Venetian plaster 50

Wainscoting 26, 30, 126

Wall Mounted 93

Walls 48–55

Water 12, 14, 18, 45–46, 48–51, 68, 70, 76, 78, 82, 84, 86–88, 97

Williams, Tennessee 53

Window(s). 22, 34, 40, 45, 52, 74, 82, 86, 128, 134

Window coverings 14, 22, 33–34

Wright, Frank Lloyd 73